T0348849

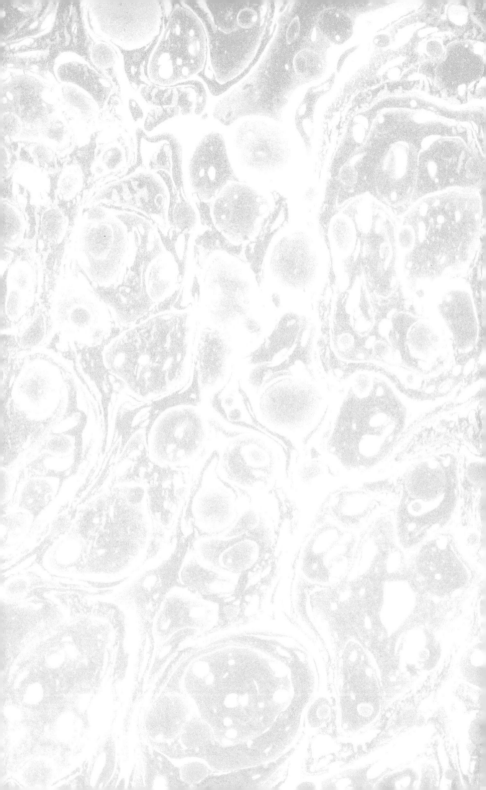

# First
*and Lasting*
Impressions

# First *and Lasting* Impressions

## SKETCHES FROM FORTY YEARS IN POLITICS AND PUBLIC LIFE

# Frank Field

### INTRODUCTION BY ANNE DE COURCY

UNICORN

# Contents

# Foreword

## DANIEL SANCHEZ

I spent three years working as Frank's assistant and researcher until his death. I saw him almost every day. Despite confronting the immense challenge of surviving cancer, his unwavering commitment to others never faltered. He continued to serve on the boards of Cool Earth and Feeding Britain, as well as the Frank Field Education Trust. The challenges of climate change, ending hunger and improving life chances were at the core of his mission.

Having previously declined honours, he accepted a seat in the House of Lords in 2020 to have a platform from which to hold the government to account through frequent Written Questions. It was at this point that our journey together would begin. I came to know not just the brilliant mind behind this book, but the remarkable man who left an indelible mark on everyone he encountered. I write this with a profound sense of honour, but also of great loss.

In October 2021, it was announced that Frank was terminally ill and had spent time in a hospice. Messages of support poured out but, as we know now, this wasn't to be the end. He was given a new lease of life by the Royal Trinity Hospice in Clapham who reformulated his medication; enormous thanks are due to them. Frank was determined to make the most of his extra time here and so we quickly got to work. First, he completed the herculean task of writing his memoir, which was published in 2023. Our attention then turned to this volume, *First and Lasting Impressions*, though this was to prove much more challenging as his health deteriorated.

The original idea was for *First and Lasting Impressions* to be published in lieu of a full memoir or set of diaries. It was to be inspired by the structure and style of John Aubrey's *Brief Lives* – a collection of short biographies on well-known figures written by Aubrey in the late decades of the seventeenth century. Frank believed he could tell an interesting story of his career in public life through his encounters; by penning portraits of significant persons he had engaged with at various stages of his career. The idea, and work on the draft, pre-dated my time in his office, with some content stemming from contemporaneous diaries. However, this was clearly not nearly enough to form a coherent, publishable piece of work, and it was thanks to Andrew Forsey, the one-time head of Frank's parliamentary office in the House of Commons, that a series of substantial 'essays' were found, allowing for the revival of this project and for it to start in earnest. My heartfelt thanks are due to Johnny and Catherine Armitage. It was only because of their generosity that I was able to work with and support Frank in this way during this crucial stage of his life.

The next hurdle we faced was finding a publisher for this work. It was in the summer of 2022 that I contacted Ian Strathcarron at Unicorn Publishing. Approaching him was eased by the fact that he also sits in the House of Lords. To my delight and relief, Ian was just as enthusiastic about the project as I was. It was not, however, just a question of emailing Unicorn a draft – some of the manuscript only existed on papers that I came across in Frank's London flat. This included his short introduction, and a great deal of care had to be taken as they were the only copies I possessed.

My daily interactions with Frank offered me a unique window into the life of a man who shaped policy, sometimes even in the most unconventional of ways. On receiving a leak of classified papers from the late Malcolm Wicks, Frank, as director of the CPAG, wrote an article exposing James Callaghan's plans to U-turn on the introduction of child benefit. This led to public outrage and frantic investigation by the government to find the perpetrators of this leak. Frank kept it a secret for thirty-eight years and went to great lengths to ensure Malcolm was never exposed as he would surely be charged under the Official Secrets Act. The aftermath resulted in Frank's phones being tapped, and he was certain his flat had been bugged after a mysterious break-in.

Frank possessed a gift for understanding and connecting with people just as well as with the public figures he encountered. His ability to see beyond the surface and capture the true essence of these individuals is evident in the nuanced portraits he presents in *First and Lasting Impressions*. As we reviewed manuscripts and revisited memories, certain recollections would give him particular pleasure. A particular standout was his 'We're not paid by the hour' rebuttal to the late George Carman QC. He would tell close friends this story with a smirk on his face. You could tell he was proud of it.

And so, dear reader, it gives me great pleasure to invite you to delve into this work. Frank's insights and observations provide a lasting contribution to our understanding of public life and leadership. For those who knew him, and for those who will come to know him through these pages, his wisdom will continue to resonate, for Frank understood that politics was about compromise and working with political opponents to bring about real change. I am confident that his stories, rich with detail and imbued with his characteristic wit and wisdom, are a testament to his enduring impact on British politics.

# Introduction

## ANNE DE COURCY

Frank Field, Lord Field of Birkenhead, CH, PC, died a few months before this book was published. His memorial service was at Holy Trinity, Sloane Street, by invitation only, as that is what Frank had requested. This meant that many of the congregation knew each other – and all were connected with Frank in some way.

Connection was, in fact, one of Frank's great gifts, for his real genius was as a human being; and it is to the credit of the House of Commons that its members – except for the most committed ideologues – recognised this: these portraits of those he knew well span both parties as well as many professions, as did his host of friends. An almost lifelong member of the Labour Party, he was liked and trusted by many Conservative MPs, indeed, regularly having tea with Mrs Thatcher; it was Frank who told the Iron Lady at the end of her third term that it was time for her to go (and support John Major) because he felt none of her own party would be brave enough to do so.

I knew Frank in the latter part of his life, and can only say that, when we met, I was immediately struck by that very rare quality: sheer goodness, which somehow exuded from him like an aura. You felt immediately and warmly at ease in his presence, as though you would not be judged for trivial lapses or foolish errors but only for what you really were. Perhaps this aspect of his personality came from working for others all his life, rather than himself. This did not mean he was not capable of crisp and sometimes severe judgements: his view of Gordon Brown, for example, was of a man unpleasant to the point of being deranged. 'I vowed that if it was the last thing I did, I would try to prevent this man from being prime minister. Another failed objective,' he once said.

Although inextricably linked to his solidly Labour constituency of Birkenhead, Frank had begun life from quite a different stance. He was born (in July 1942) in Edmonton, the second of the three sons of a factory worker father and a mother who was a primary school welfare worker, both of whom voted Conservative; and young Frank duly joined the Conservative Party.

The first hint that he might leave the fold came with the 1959 election when, as a fifteen-year-old grammar school boy, he found himself captivated both by the manner and by the graceful acceptance of defeat by Hugh Gaitskell, then Leader of the Labour Party. It was also a signifier of the future, for although Frank would fight relentlessly for causes he cherished, he also believed in the moral elegance of accepting one's fate without complaint.

As an undergraduate at the University of Hull, reading Economics, he left the Conservative Party in 1960 because of his opposition to apartheid in South Africa – almost sixty years later, he left Labour for the same root cause, racism, citing antisemitism in the party. He had held the safe Labour seat of Birkenhead for forty years, for which he was selected after ten years running the party-neutral Child Poverty Action Group (CPAG) – a decade that saw him making many cross-party friends.

One such friend was Margaret Thatcher, whom he met when lobbying her on behalf of the CPAG. 'Shall I follow you, Prime Minister?' he asked as she emerged from the Chamber. 'People usually do,' was her reply, as she led the way into the L-shaped Prime Minister's

Room behind the Speaker's Chair. There was whisky on offer ('she herself was reputed to be able to drink anyone under the table'). Frank returned home a fan. 'It was the power to decide and drive through decisions that so appealed to me.'

They got to know each other so well that it was Frank, not a member of her own party, who told her that it was time to go, in a late, late night meeting in which he folded her in his arms, saying that she had always been kind to him, now it was his turn to be kind to her – by telling her the truth. After he had finished, he was smuggled out by the back door: TV cameras were parked at the front. Two days later, she resigned.

There are glimpses both of the finagling that goes on behind the scenes and the nuts and bolts of the sheer business of getting anything done, sometimes with unexpected side-effects. During the inquiry into the disappearance of the Maxwell pension funds, the Maxwell brothers, Ian and Kevin, were investigated on television, with Ian being particularly well defended. In Birkenhead, Frank's agent was bombarded by calls from the constituency's top-flight criminals demanding to know the name of Ian's QC.

There are fascinating vignettes. Here is Frank 'getting slightly squiffy' with Enoch Powell, as he lobbies, along with three Tory MPs, for an order for Cammell Laird shipyards; here he is being gripped by the lapels and shaken by a raging Gordon Brown shouting, 'I thought you were my friend, my friend, my friend.' Here is Edward Heath, whose terseness was then legendary, taking all of 45 seconds to answer the five questions Frank had put to him. concerning the CPAG, with the other 44 minutes and 15 seconds allotted for the meeting taken up by tea and awkward conversation, during which Heath talked exclusively about sailing. But then, wondered Frank, what other Leader of the Opposition had won the Sydney to Hobart, one of the world's toughest ocean races?

And here is a Labour Party meeting in Joan Lestor's constituency of Eton and Slough (safe to say, the Slough element preponderated). Staged in the huge, smoke-filled hall of Slough Technical College, the whole evening was marked by violence. Harold Wilson was to speak but was still en route, and the hall was so packed that 'people were climbing through the huge metal frame windows. As they did so, others, inside, closed the windows leaving the late entrants literally hanging by their fingertip.' As two rival groups within the hall fought each other ('fists flew') news came that the Prime Minister was further delayed and Frank, the warm-up man, had to continue speaking 'to keep them happy'. When Wilson finally arrived, he was struck in the eye by a missile; Frank poured a jug of cold water over his face to cool the pain down, remarking, 'Pity our fast bowlers aren't as accurate' (the Test match was going badly for England).

Frank was sustained throughout his life by his strong Christian faith. It was this – his adherence to doing, or trying to do, the morally right thing rather than loyalty to the party line – that accounted for many of the 'contradictions' or apparent *volte faces* in his career; after being co-opted on to the Synod, for instance, his unwavering support for women priests led to his being blocked by a powerful anti-group. But always his main focus was on the poor and the deprived, the children born into poverty or those who had slipped into it through no fault of their own. For those who could not fight for themselves, he fought, and fearlessly.

# Preface

FRANK FIELD

*Why I Write*

Never trust a politician. And I'm no exception. I always refused to write any form of autobiography or memoir, as I lack the courage and objectivity shown in William Waldegrave's *A Different Kind of Weather*. William sets a standard for any autobiographer to aim at. This effort, therefore, comes with a serious political health warning.

Politicians write autobiographies to justify and inflate their importance. You, the reader, are the jury. They also write, they hope, to engage and amuse. I have chosen snapshots of my life that aim to do both. Again, the jury makes the call.

I have written in the style of Aubrey's *Brief Lives* as a close friend suggested, knowing that I would not write a straight up and down version of events that people call a 'life'. A suggestion of a half-way house was seized upon. *First and Lasting Impressions* holds many attractions for me.

My first years in Birkenhead were horrible. The town was Militant's epicentre. Peter Taaffe, their theorist, was born locally, and the town was to fall to them. Michael Foot once said that if Birkenhead fell, then so would the Labour Party.

Our fight in Birkenhead, with a band of loyal supporters, was long, hard and bloody. No one in authority rushed to help, although so many people claimed success after Militant was repelled. They are liars. The lying about me during the campaign was such that I have never ceased to be amazed. Our regular party meetings would consist of me standing there while people were making the most terrible allegations. *How can they even think them up?* I wondered. Likewise, *How credible do I seem in always denying them?* Surely, we all make errors, and I was making myself ridiculous by holding to what I believed to be true.

Keeping a diary was the very last thing in the world I could do. Everything in me rebelled against keeping a record of what was going on. I just longed to get on to the next day and, possibly, victory.

It was a long time into that war against Militant before I knew I would win. No matter how feeble the national party was, there eventually came a point when I realised that being destroyed or not was in my own hands.

I had showered and was shaving before going up to Birkenhead to face the Trots yet again. I vomited into the basin. I was so afraid, once the vomit had ceased to sting in my nose, I looked into the shaving mirror. There was this pathetic sight, and I knew that I could make excuses, run away from it for the rest of my life or outface them that day in Birkenhead. And so I went up there to begin the rest of my life.

The second attraction of the *Brief Lives* approach is that I could, in an introduction to the life forces I describe in the following pages, stand back and draw out the lessons I want to hand on to those who follow me. Politics is a great career but it is only as good as the people we elect to be our representatives.

What micro and macro lessons would I draw from my political life? For 'micro' read 'people', who are the beginning and end of all good politics. I represented a proper place that had hardly changed in size since I was first elected in 1979. Representing Birkenhead was one of the great gifts that life bestowed on me but one that engaged me in an almost continuous tutorial.

Most of what I said and campaigned for had been taught to me by my constituents as they sought help, in conversations with them, or, alternatively, as they pulled around ideas I brought to the job as their MP. This little volume records some of what I learned as I tried to do politics with the brief lives recorded here.

It was in doing politics my way that I felt easiest being Birkenhead's representative in parliament. In Westminster I was pulled in different directions. I had a loyalty to the founding principles of the Labour Party, which of course was totally different from the pull of that passing pressure from the whips. These MPs have to take a day-to-day view of politics. Getting business through (if government whips) or opposing business (if they are appointed by the leader of the opposition) is a crucial part of making the governing party responsible to the electorate. We are elected on a clear manifesto, and we are judged on whether we have delivered or not on clear policy.

I would like to think conscience plays its part and often wonder whether I kid myself that this is my lodestar or whether I am irrationally driven. Here you, dear reader, must make your judgement.

In truth, I could not represent the people of Birkenhead by being their representative in any traditional sense of the term. Most importantly, I did not know what 'their' views were and whether they were momentary or persistent. There were few MPs busier than me in their constituencies, I hoped, but during my Thursday nights to Saturday afternoons in Birkenhead I heard a cacophony of views on all sorts of topics; and this symphony was modern, with an overdose of discordant notes.

Do I kid myself again on this score? Do I try to learn, but merely 'learn' to reinforce my existing views or prejudices? Was there a development of these views as I dug myself into Birkenhead and the world around us changed so much? I hope that has been discernible too.

I was a representative of Birkenhead's electorate in the sense that I stood on a programme, and voters could bring me down at the following election if they wished.

From previous electoral arithmetic, it looks as though the burghers of Birkenhead see the nature of representation in the way that I do. But I was hugely privileged. I only went into the House of Commons twice before I was elected. On one occasion I sat in the public gallery as R.A. Butler introduced a procedural committee report on reform. He talked of Pitt standing similarly at the despatch box and observing out loud that government business could only be despatched thanks to the loyalty of the thick Tory squires behind him. Rab Butler turned his face that was disfigured, in the sense that his jaw looked as though it did not belong to the rest of his head, and gave a sickly smile to those thick Tory squires. I knew from that day that he would never be prime minister. Thick they may have been, but memories they had, and such insults were easily recognisable.

I have been hugely privileged in that there have always been good enough Labour MPs to support a Labour programme or oppose a Tory one. It's only in this world of loyalty – which I rate – that I took that freedom to try to push and pull and tug at the direction of policy.

The way l tried always to get Labour in front of the curve, in this instance in the selling of council houses, was a case in point. It is in this sense that my irritant pressure fits in with the theory of 'representative and responsible government' that A.H. Birch lays out in his outstanding book that carries that same title.

Westminster, 2024

# Hugh Gaitskell

Christopher Farley[1] would entertain dinner guests by producing, and then reading from, a handwritten letter from Gaitskell requesting Farley to lay off criticising him in his column.

This information was given to me by the historian John Grigg, possibly to temper my enthusiasm for Hugh Gaitskell. John was one of the great historians of modern politics and wrote about Lloyd George's role in it. And he had been present at one such occasion when this sacred text was produced. John believed Farley's aim was to puncture what was then the overwhelming mourning among the chattering classes that Gaitskell's early death in 1963 had dealt an immeasurable blow to British politics. Here was an insight

---

1. Of the *New Left Review*

suggesting that Gaitskell's 'thin skin' meant that he lacked the sterner qualities needed by all prime ministers.

I joined the Labour Party because I so admired Gaitskell's way of doing politics. He was a Roundhead following in the Oliver Cromwell tradition. Gaitskell believed passionately in upholding principles and presenting these principles in sets of workable, everyday policies. Gaitskell's principled approach to politics did not, however, prevent him from being pragmatic in their implementation. A degree of flexibility is an essential tool in any successful politician's armoury. There were, indeed, those who thought Gaitskell inflexible in imposing a small charge for NHS teeth and glasses. Surely this ran counter to the principle of a service being free 'from cradle to grave'? I read Gaitskell's actions differently. He used the small charges to begin to confront the Labour Party and, in particular, Aneurin Bevan, who led Labour's romantic or cavalier tendency, with the unpalatable truth about health costs. But Gaitskell, no doubt, believed that this lesson on the health service could and should be read over the whole gamut of public expenditure.

It was in the lead-up to the 1959 election that I began to notice Gaitskell. I was then an active young Conservative, all of fifteen years old, and was standing on one of those steel-framed chairs with brown canvas seats in the Brentford and Chiswick Conservative Association. It was polling night. Our election result had been declared quickly and our candidate, with an increased majority, had led a posse back to watch the rest of the results come in.

There was no question about the overall result. The trend was clear from the first results, and long before the cameras switched to Leeds Town Hall where the counts for that city's seats were being declared. The central camera was on Gaitskell and he was about to concede defeat to his political enemies. He did so with an extraordinary degree of beauty and grace. It was possible, even from a flickering black and white picture, to read his emotions, and to discern the inescapable tiredness that sweeps across the face of all those when defeat finally stalks and traps its prey.

I was mesmerised. I was new to politics and had never before seen such raw emotion. If only I could have performed like that when life's inevitable defeats struck me. These impressions were rudely interrupted by crude shouting at the TV by our newly elected MP who was standing on a chair next to me at the back of the room. It would have been difficult to conjure up a greater contrast between Gaitskell's graceful acceptance of defeat and the vulgar triumphalism of the man we had just elected in Brentford and Chiswick.[2] Despite my party loyalty, I found I wanted to shove my neighbour off his perch. But, unlike Gaitskell, I lacked courage. The crudities continued as I remained pathetically motionless and silent.

I saw Gaitskell speak only once at university. A crowd of undergraduates had pushed their way into Hull University's assembly room and, sitting there, isolated on an absurdly elevated platform, was the distinguished party of Hull MPs, and the great man himself. Although I was by then besotted by Gaitskell's leadership, I cannot remember a word of what he said on that occasion. I do, however, remember only too well his upper-middle class manner of speaking and his somewhat clipped sentences. I also remember he wore a brown suit and brown shoes as my grandfather did when dressed in his Sunday best. It was this side of Gaitskell, that brown suit and brown shoes, which was so attacked by our class-based English snobbery. Gentlemen didn't dress like my beloved grandfather who had been a milkman. But I loved everything about my grandfather, including those tears that ran down his face, that so frightened me, when he talked about the First World War – or rather, refused to talk about that war to end all wars. In some ways, therefore, I identified those qualities in Gaitskell: his refusal to play the class

---

2. Dudley Smith, who lost Brentford and Chiswick in 1966, became the member for Warwick and Leamington in 1968

game and his empathy with the rough hand that had been dealt to so many working-class people.

My other memory of Gaitskell is much more significant. It centred on his stand, lonely at first, against the Tories' restriction on black immigrants. He fixed my interest. Here were the politics of principle played with verve and great skill. The Macmillan government had panicked over rising immigration from the Commonwealth, and Macmillan did panic rather well. Their Immigration Bill had been rushed in, restricting black immigrants only. It was the lowering of the portcullis against people who believed this was also their mother country, and whose young men had fought alongside us in two world wars that struck me as being so unjust. The worst type of ingratitude, where one country strikes at another that had proved its worth by sending its young men to defend and to die in defence of a far-away country that was seen as the mother of the Empire.

Gaitskell's stand appalled all too many of his colleagues, who argued for caution. The polls showed overwhelming support for the bill, and then as now, Labour supporters were as keen for the measure as their Tory counterparts. But Gaitskell's response showed his great strength as a political leader, more so, I think, than his great 'Fight, fight and fight again' speech against unilateralism. On that occasion he had the vast majority of the country and most of his immediate colleagues on his side. Not so on immigration.

The Immigration Bill, Gaitskell argued, was as morally wrong as it would be self-defeating. Here was the ground on which Gaitskell stood. In his main House of Commons speech against the measure Gaitskell outlined what he saw as the natural rhythm to immigration. When job vacancies were plenty, and employers were scouring the labour market for workers, the message went home to Jamaica and the surrounding islands that work was plentiful. People came. The reverse was also true. No jobs – don't come. Yet, by sounding the trumpet in the manner the government had done, the restrictions they were imposing generated the rush of West Indians that their restrictions were being imposed to prevent. As the bill was going through Parliament, ships were leaving the Caribbean Islands and offering up so many of their most energetic sons and daughters to their mother country. Hence, Gaitskell argued, the crisis the government wished to combat was one of its own making. Much later, the Oxford geography professor Ceri Peach showed in a learned tome just how right Gaitskell's analysis was of the ebb and flow of immigration.

But, as in all Gaitskell's politics, it was not only the accuracy of his analysis that counted: what mattered most was its moral force. It was the fundamental injustice of singling out people by their colour that Gaitskell so hated. From the newspaper reports (I was then a reader of the *News Chronicle*) I gained a sense of Gaitskell's rage at the moral iniquity of the measure. By the end of its parliamentary passage, Gaitskell had swung public opinion behind him. Although initially isolated, he believed in the fundamental decency and fair mindedness of the British people. He fought on this platform. And won.

I was never to see Gaitskell after this great triumph. It was through the radio news reports that I, and no doubt so many more, prepared for the worst. I remember being in my room at university listening to my wonderful 'sit up and beg' radio, with its walnut case and real valves, gleaning what information I could about Gaitskell's declining health. I willed not to happen what I feared would. After a few days of bulletins, the end came. Gaitskell was dead.

I have never been more affected by the death of a person I only knew from his public life, and I must say Gaitskell was one of my biggest influences. I still miss his particular political magic a lifetime later. And after living through the Blair and Brown governments I think Henry Farley misjudged his man. I longed for a Labour leader who leads from the front, clear on his or her moral compass to decide the day-to-day issues, and for whom focus groups were an unnecessary and misleading substitute for principle.

# Jack Jones

*'Vera will always fit you into the car with me as I move between meetings.'*

T his was just one act of kindness that Jack Jones showed to me
while I was lobbying on behalf of the CPAG. He was then, in
the late 1960s, the most powerful trade union leader in the land at
a time when trade unions appeared to be more powerful than the
elected Labour government. He was a Liverpudlian, though I had no
idea then that I would seek to represent in Parliament an area from
which he came. He was wonderfully urbane, gentle, and determined
to help CPAG in its campaign to counter poverty. He was a proper
person, serious in intent in defending the poor. There was none of the
showmanship that so often, if not always, comes to someone wielding
great power and he had not opted for a lifestyle that took him away

from how his membership lived. There was no hint of gesture politics. On every issue on which he gave his word, he delivered.

Jack was at the time General Secretary of the Transport and General Workers' Union (TGWU) and Vera, his long-time secretary, was equally helpful and supportive. Without her interest I wouldn't have had access in the way I did to the most powerful person in the land. Jack's diary was full, as befits a man that was ruling Britain indirectly through a Labour Cabinet. I would phone Vera whenever I needed to talk to Jack and ask his advice. She would tell me what his movements were that day and ask when I would be free to be picked up in the TGWU car that would at that time be taking Jack between meetings. Into the car I would get and raise my agenda issues with Jack. His driver was crucial to the well-running of this operation. When my conversation with Jack was finished, he would detour if necessary and put me down at the nearest Underground station so that I could make my way back to CPAG's base in Macklin Street.

During these conversations Jack would advise me on the immediate agenda that CPAG was trying to raise. He was a member of the Trade Union Congress's (TUC's) then most powerful committee – the Economic Committee – and naturally the most powerful member of it. It was through this committee and the General Council that Jack wielded the authority of the trade union movement and from that base through into the decision-making machinery of the Labour government. Central to my concern was the case, and urgency, of raising family allowances.

Jack would advise what kind of memorandum we should produce, when we should produce it and how we should get it on to the key agendas of the relevant TUC committees. If the submission was not coming to his committee, he would keep an eye on its progress. But he told me more.

A lobbyist has a number of traditional approaches available to them. If the lobbying is of a sustained character, then two such approaches are the writing of detailed letters in order to gain a clear commitment, or a face-to-face meeting. These approaches, useful when relevant, were hopeless when, say, there was a report of a dramatic turn of events affecting the poor in the evening or overnight news. How should I react in these circumstances when trying to influence and help persuade the general secretaries of the various unions that action was needed to support or warn the Labour government? What should be a lobbyist's response when contact was required immediately?

Jack's advice was clear. At that stage of the game it was too late for general secretaries to be influenced by any letters from me. Vera would tell me if there was a relevant trade union meeting that Jack would be attending with his senior colleagues. Many of the general secretaries were picked up in their cars and taken to their TUC meeting before ever darkening the doorway of their office. Jack told me, however, that all of them read the *Guardian* as they were driven to the TUC building, and this should be used, if at all possible, as the means of providing me with an opportunity to brief all the general secretaries as I would have done by letter had the time scale allowed.

The *Guardian*, to its great credit, played ball. The reporters knew on some occasions why I was putting such emphasis on a particular story and its urgency. Of course there was some self-interest here, as they would be breaking news. But the reporters were also aware of their role in furthering an agenda of which they approved. The *Guardian* never failed in this respect and played a hugely important part in CPAG's link with the most powerful person in the country, his colleagues and the organisation, the TUC, through which he worked.

In retirement Jack spent his last years looking after his wife who had become frail with Alzheimer's. Barbara Wootton, a well-known sociologist and later Baroness Wootton of Abinger, CH, once remarked to me that, as we get older, we become more like ourselves.

Jack, in my experience, remained as I had always found him. He never pulled rank, but attempted to disappear from public life. He was unsuccessful – naturally. He was pulled back to lead a pensioners' revolt, as President of the National Pensioners Convention. He did so with aplomb and immediately became again a towering figure on the campaigning scene.

After Jack died, he was 'exposed' as being a communist spy. What was the background to Jack's exposé? The stimulus to collect information on people like Jack came from Mrs T, who was fishing around to have what she regarded as conclusive evidence on trade union subversives. In the authorised history of MI5, *The Defence of the Realm*, written by Professor Christopher Andrew, who was given complete access to MI5's files, Jack had last received money from the KGB via his case officer in 1985. The case officer happened to be working for British intelligence! The information that Jack supplied was trade union and Labour Party papers.

I was totally taken aback as I had seen him as a working-class nationalist. I argued with myself the mitigating factor, that Jack in his youth had gone to Spain to fight for the working-class Republican cause and had seen what a fascist regime was like. His anger at the working class losing out in life had burnt quietly and powerfully within him.

But I still feel that certain loyalties are primary and that one such loyalty is to one's country rather than to a set of ideas or ideologies. While Jack's passing of papers to the Soviet Union presumably proved ineffective enough, it was still wrong. Yet I do not want to forget the other side of Jack's character, with his extraordinary kindness to me as a lobbying novice, trying to build up a range of skills that could be deployed more effectively on behalf of poorer people. As a tutor he was second to none in this role. Thank goodness his tutorial skills were way beyond those of a spy.

# Harold Wilson

*'I've been hit,' the Prime Minister groaned, clutching his right eye.
'You can't have been,' I replied. 'The missiles are coming
from the other side of the hall.'*

It was my second meeting with Harold Wilson. This time the
Prime Minister had been delayed in Reading and I was one of the
speakers at his last port of call – at Joan Lestor's (then Labour MP for
Eton and Slough) mega rally at Slough Technical College. Staged in
its huge hall, the whole evening was marked by violence. A thousand
people were present, too many of them shouting and screaming at
one other, and I had been let out for my second public meeting.

I couldn't properly focus on the back of the hall; such was the
density of the trapped tobacco smoke. The hall was packed to over-

capacity. People were climbing up to enter through the huge metal frame windows. As they did, others, inside, closed the windows, leaving the late entrants literally hanging by their fingertips.

Two small bands of opposing supporters rushed around the hall diving into groups of their opponents. Fists flew before the assailants withdrew. This was the cue for the opposing raiding party to leave their starting blocks and attack groups of their opponents. I had never witnessed before, or since, such naked hostility between Tory and Labour supporters.

As I viewed this violence, my thoughts drifted to the assassination scene of Bobby Kennedy. Was it like this I wondered? I was the youngest Labour candidate in the 1966 general election and fighting the neighbouring seat to Joan's, the rock-solid Tory Buckinghamshire South constituency. I had been absurdly allotted the role of keeping the audience happy as they awaited the Prime Minister's entry.

My hands shook as I turned over to my last page. The chairman was watching and passed me a note. 'PM delayed in Reading. Keep speaking.' I did as best I could. Having a fat lot of experience, I somewhat pathetically began my speech again. Another note arrived with the same instructions. So, I continued to speak from what I had prepared and the phrases, as they were spoken, for goodness knows how long, echoed as though they were being drilled into my head. I continued, only to be reminded by another note with the same instructions.

I don't know how long I ended up speaking for. It seemed like hours. As was the reaction from at least part of the assembled crowd, much of which was seething up and down before me. Then, between the intermittent acts of violence, an unexpected silence fell upon the hall. This was seized upon by one Tory heckler, with a yelling out in a sergeant major type of voice, 'I'm bored!'

I jumped back.

'So am I.' The hall erupted in applause and cheering. I was away, picking up themes from the audience. When the Prime Minister arrived, I was sorry to have to hand over to him.

The violence continued, shouting and screaming, with the opposing parties equally active. I was sitting next to the Prime Minister, on his right side. It didn't seem that long into his session before he turned to me to say, 'I'm hit.' He was rubbing his right eye. 'You can't have been,' I replied. 'The missiles are coming from the other side of the hall.'

He continued to speak. I can't remember what he was going on about. I was too excited and gripped by the chaos before me. I had never witnessed anything like it. He then sat down and quietly told me that his eye was burning. Pushing his head back I picked up the nearest jug of water and poured it gently over his eye. He dried himself with his handkerchief.

The chairman, as they were then called, asked if there was a doctor in the hall. There was. The PM went off stage and Joan Lestor gave one of her soul-raising speeches on why we needed to re-elect the Labour government.

Then, in deafening noise, the rally was brought to an end. The stage party filed off and I went to see the Prime Minister. He was sitting in a side room. He thanked me for my actions. A stink bomb had hit him in his eye. He was grateful for the jug of water being poured over his eye, which was now fine.

'Pity our fast bowlers are not as accurate as that missile thrower,' I remarked. We were doing very badly in that year's Test series. Wilson laughed and wished me luck in getting into the House. On the radio early next morning, the newsreader reported that the Prime Minister had dismissed the attack, commenting that it was a pity that our fast bowlers couldn't match the accuracy of his stink bomb assassin.

My first public outing as a speaker had also involved Harold Wilson. Although, this time, he was thankfully present throughout the meeting. The regional Labour Party had arranged a rally in

Buckinghamshire and I was to end the prime ministerial rally with a brief thank-you.

I was thinking about what I would say in the week before that Saturday date. I ached with nerves, as I still do before speaking or broadcasting. *What could anyone possibly want to hear from me?* I kept thinking, and was doing so when I sat down one lunchtime that week in an eel pie shop near to where I worked. Two pensioners were already at the table and in conversation. I sat down beside them. They nodded and continued. They were, not unnaturally, complaining how difficult it was to make ends meet. The conversation was on the task of stretching their pensions, and it continued until one of them remarked that she would have thought that Labour would have done more for pensioners. The other turned to her and said, 'Yes, but I feel much safer now Old 'Arold's there.'

I had my theme. We were making a good start as a government and wanted to do more, but, even so, the most vulnerable voters felt safer 'now that Old 'Arold's there in Number 10'. At this point my speech gained lift-off due to a heckler.

'Not so much of the "Old 'Arold", thank you.'

'My two pensioners had a name for people like you,' I retorted.

The audience began to laugh as the quips came quick and fast, and the Prime Minister, with his unlit pipe in his mouth, laughed along as he prepared to leave.

Then up jumped Bob Maxwell. He was local MP for the town where the rally was being held, but had not been billed with any part. Rushing up to the Prime Minister, he grabbed the mic. 'Let me tell you,' he roared, 'about my lobbying the Prime Minister.'

Goodness knows quite what the issue was. I was transfixed looking at the PM. By now Wilson was holding the top end of his pipe, which remained firmly in his mouth, and he was twisting it around, holding the base of the pipe by his teeth. Anger swept across his face as he continued to push his pipe anti-clockwise, while holding the base of the pipe by his teeth. He will break his teeth, I thought, if Maxwell continues like this.

For me it was the most wonderful lesson of how not to lobby. Maxwell may have picked up a few home votes for ranting on about some local issue, but he was going nowhere, I thought. Which was true, as events turned out years later; or was not quite true, depending on your views about the afterlife.

# Anthony Crosland

Iwas dazzled by his handsomeness, and the confidence Crosland emitted as if from every pore of his body.

It was his sharpness of thought and clear abundance of brains that were so attractive to a grammar school boy trying to weigh the role of ideas in shaping and driving politics. There was more than a touch of intellectual magic in Anthony Crosland's *The Future of Socialism*. It was first published in 1956 and, although I was aware of it, I didn't open its covers until I was in the second year at university.

It was, however, the bible for revisionists in the Labour Party and I thought of myself then as part of this vanguard. Now I realise that revisionism alone is not enough. But then we saw our role in making Labour intelligible to voters, and for voters to see us as a solution to their lives' difficulties; helping them meet their aspirations rather than adding to their lives' difficulties and blocking their aspirations. It was by his pen that Crosland wielded his implements for he was never an outstanding Speaker. A series of articles in *Encounter*, or appearing as Fabian Tracts, or, of course, that book of his, were the many vehicles by which he wielded influence within the Labour movement.

The first time I clapped eyes on the great man was at a party in the early 1960s in the somewhat drab atmosphere of Transport House. Here was the home of the mighty T&G Union (TGWU) built to pre-eminence by the skill of Ernie Bevin, but housing also the Labour Party's headquarters. The offices, like the Labour Party, had seen better days and were badly in need of a major facelift.

The room was sparsely populated and Ray Gunter – soon to be become the Minister for Labour in Harold Wilson's 1964 government – shuffled around, his neck bulging over his collar and puffed out by his own self-importance. Then the atmosphere dramatically changed. In swept Crosland with his new wife Susan. I was dazzled by their handsomeness and the confidence Crosland emitted as if from every pore of his body. He knew he was good and took no trouble to hide it. His was a confidence of the kind I had not witnessed before.

I saw Crosland only a few times after that, although he seemed ever present through his regular stream of publications. At the Fabian School where I first met Shirley Williams and her husband Bernard, and Bill and Silvia Rodgers, all Crosland's abiding characteristics were well on display. Casually but smartly dressed he may have been, but the natural superiority remained, reinforced I noticed this time by a slight nasal drawl that he used to emphasise the key importance of what he was saying. It operated as underlining on a written page.

Crosland was one of those individuals whose position in the Labour hierarchy owed more to the quality of his brains than was generally the case. But even he benefited from a protector, which was so important in a political career as in so many others.

Crosland was helped on his way by Hugh Dalton[1] who did much to promote younger, super-intellectual and attractive young Labour Party men, help them into their parliamentary seats and then up the party's greasy pole.

Crosland was also helped by the timing of his publication *The Future of Socialism*, which came out at a time when Gaitskell's revisionist drive needed a political text to underpin his radical departures.

It is a matter of debate how influential Crosland's book was to this revolution in Labour Party affairs that Gaitskell was trying to enact. This debate is interesting for the contemporary historian but is a side matter for us. Whatever the answer to this conundrum it misses the main point of the role of the big book in the movement of ideas.

How many of those confessing themselves to be socialists have read Marx's *Das Kapital*, even those who profess to be promoting his ideas. Likewise, while record sales have been recorded for Stephen Hawking's books on the big bang and the theory of black holes, how many of these books have been actually read? Yet armies of disciples propagate what they believe to be the master's message.

So, too, with Crosland's great book. It gave us revisionist disciples greater confidence to engage the enemy who we all too often saw as being in the same party. But when differences between parties, let alone within, are as small as they now are it is hard to capture the intellectual clout and moral authority that Crosland's work gave to our particular wing of Labour's foot soldiers.

I read Crosland's great text during my second year of university. My life was changed as much as it could be, during that year, but not by reading this text. I had just been given – if that is the correct term for it – a tutorial by Trevor Smith.[2] Trevor taught largely by humour

1. Labour Party economist and politician and Chancellor of the Exchequer 1945–7.
2. Later the Liberal Democrat peer Lord Smith of Clifton.

and my sides were frequently aching with laughter. He held an essay of mine, and out of the blue he asked why I didn't work and make the most of the brains I had.

That special magic touch that all good teachers possess – and seeing its effect must be one of teaching's great rewards and fulfilments – touched me as if God had commanded a thunderbolt down upon me. For, from that day since, I've worked, ever seeking new ways of being more effective and more productive – which I sometimes believe to be one and the same thing. This was at the time when Bryan Magee published *The New Radicalism* in which he wonderfully sidestepped the bone-aching exercise of having to prove to fellow adherents that one was a true socialist.

A Radio 3 programme came to Hull for a student–tutor discussion with Magee. Here was a class act to put Crosland in the shade. Only long afterwards, when we crossed paths as Members in the House of Commons, did I begin to realise how gigantic was, in Denis Healey's phrase, his hinterland. But listening to Magee I saw for the first time what Labour traditionalists feared from us revisionists.

Where would the revisionism stop? If you are prepared, say, to throw nationalisation overboard for that slippery eel-like conception of equality, where would it all end?

Crosland never grappled with this issue to my satisfaction, nor was I that happy with his unqualified insistence that high public expenditure was a key sign of socialism in action. I felt it was more of a fig leaf to cover his own ideological nakedness. More dangerously, it also built into Labour Party thinking that somewhat cavalier attitude of the Blair/Brown era of 'spend, spend and spend again'. Quantity only became the right strategy, while outcomes for that expenditure were rarely considered.

Yet, in the great clash of ideas in the Callaghan/Healey era I believe Crosland was right. When Labour couldn't pay the bills any more the International Monetary Fund (IMF) marched into town to perform their particular form of economic black magic. Crosland led the counter-offensive against the IMF demands of swingeing public expenditure cuts. His Cabinet allies, even though correct in their analysis, proved a poor political match against the heavy bruisers of Healey and Callaghan.

Crosland lusted after a job at the Treasury but that post, when it became vacant, went to his great rival, Roy Jenkins. The Foreign Office's main office was open to him although, unknown to all of us, his time was fast running out.

Crosland's end, in 1977, was as dramatic as they come. A massive stroke soon led to a catatonic state. Susan described how as Crosland slowly sunk, she climbed into his hospital bed to hold the person she had so loved. What an end. Her action became known only when she began marketing her biography. The announcement of Crosland's death was a moving display. David Lipsey had worked with Crosland in Opposition as what was called a 'chocolate solider'. The non-charitable Rowntree Trust had given the Opposition money for Shadow Secretaries of State to employ political advisers.

David played this role and, like others, was later taken into government by their political masters and mistresses. Outside the Radcliffe Infirmary in Oxford, where Crosland died, David stepped before the TV cameras. He made the mournful announcement of Crosland's death with tears running down his face. For someone to have engendered such loyalty and affection says much of the politician we all too rarely saw. I have never met David – he's now a life peer – without thinking of that proud exhibition of love and dignity he displayed before those cameras.

# Iain Macleod

*'Would you mind repeating what you*
*have just said so that I can record it?'*

In 1967 I had asked for a meeting with Iain Macleod, the Tory Shadow Chancellor. This followed publication of the report *Poverty in the Labour Government*, which had begun its life as 'The Poor Get Poorer Under Labour'. The pre-Budget report had argued for an increase in family allowances as the best means open to a government by which to counter child poverty and the additional disadvantages poorer families had experienced since the 1967 devaluation of the pound.

In attempting to make the CPAG a cross-party lobby, I made sure that we did not simply lobby the Labour Party, but the other parties as well, their backbench committees and their party researchers.

By trial and error, we built up a rather impressive lobby organisation, and yet we somehow remained a charity.

After delivering our memorandum to Crossman, then Leader of the House of Commons, I had directed a copy to Iain Macleod and to John Pardoe, the Liberals' clever and competitive Treasury spokesman. I asked for a meeting with Macleod and didn't wait long for a reply. Macleod had a wonderful political bearing and was then the main carrier of the One Nation message from the Tory benches.

The appointed day arrived and Peter Townsend[1] and I met Macleod in a London hotel room. He sat in one of those standard winged chairs that, covered in velvet, became a feature of so many residential care homes. In front of him was a small round coffee table on which rested our memorandum.

Macleod quizzed us on parts of the manifesto, pushing us on questions of fact and checking the calculations. He never once referred to the memorandum, but his questions were usually prefaced by 'Page...', whatever the page was. He spent quite a long time on the ways open to government to eliminate poverty, which were listed towards the close of our document. He appeared not only extremely knowledgeable, but genuinely interested in what could be done.

I was mesmerised by the Shadow Chancellor's appearance. He sat somewhat hunch-backed and unable to move without pain. I had seen him perform in the House when some kindly figure had persuaded the powers that be to give me a place in what is called 'the box' under the public gallery. This places the observer on the same level as MPs but, unlike the MPs who faced one other, occupiers of the box face the Speaker. It was almost as if one was a Member of Parliament oneself.

Macleod was in traditional mode as he roused his own side and attempted to demolish the government's case. But it was obvious

---

1. Campaigner and later Chairman of the Child Action Poverty Group

that he had lost much of his mobility on one side of his body. It appeared as though his neck was locked. For him to look away from the Speaker and direct himself either to his own side or to the furthest Opposition benches required him to swing the whole of his body around. This immobility was pronounced during our meeting, as it had been during the Commons' performance, which ended in the uproar Macleod had always intended. Members on his own side yelled and some waved their order papers. Labour MPs cried derision. But no order papers were waved on this occasion, and our memorandum was left undisturbed on the coffee table.

During our discussion, Macleod commented on the case against means tests. A central argument then was of their low take-up, as the poor disliked being singled out in this way. It was much later that I took this whole debate upmarket by developing the poverty trap argument – that winning a wage increase could actually result, with tax and loss of means-tested benefit, in a worker becoming worse off.

Then, all of a sudden, Macleod concluded our meeting with the simple statement that he had been convinced. He would increase family allowances should he become Chancellor after the election. It was the first time that I had been at a meeting when the political kaleidoscope had been so shaken, and in such a quick dramatic way.

Had I misheard him? I swallowed and asked, 'Would you mind repeating what you've just said so that I can record it?'

My empty coffee cup was shaking as I tried to balance it with the notebook I had brought with me. My arm and hand seemed to grow paralysed with the excitement of this political breakthrough. *Labour will have to act now*, I kept telling myself. I tried to drive these ideas out of my head and, equally, drive my hand across the page to record this simple, but for us the most dramatic, of all breakthroughs.

At last, a tiny element of control reasserted itself and I managed to write 'FA' with an arrow pointing upwards. Macleod had been watching this extraordinary effort and looked kindly on.

Peter and I couldn't wait to get outside. It was the only time that I literally jumped up and down with excitement. Peter's face was a mass of smiles. If only I had attended more than a single football match with my brothers at Stamford Bridge, I might have learned some of the whistles to sound out great joy as the penalty ball goes into the net. The Labour goal was now open to us. Labour, I believed – sadly wrongly – would have to react in a more positive way than simply picking up the ball and disgruntledly running off in the opposite direction.

The competition between both parties over their intent for helping poorer families was what I had aimed for. The new stage in our lobbying war had well and truly opened, but not in the way I expected, nor with the expected outcomes for Tories or Labour.

# Richard Crossman

*'Go on and publish it. No one will believe you.' 'That's precisely what we're going to do.* The Times *have copy of our memorandum now.'*

Dick Crossman was a powerful figure in every sense of the term. He was large in stature, had a booming voice (rather like Hugh Dalton) but also had a huge muscular intellect. He must have been the cleverest person intellectually in the Wilson government, although not the most original of thinkers. That title surely goes to Anthony Crosland. Crossman was a philosophy tutor and taught Plato and Aristotle at Oxford before coming into Parliament for one of the Coventry seats.

He had been a Bevanite, which now seems tame enough given what has happened in the Labour Party as of recent, but that presented then a real challenge to the right-leaning Labour leadership of the late 1940s and early 1950s. Clement Attlee didn't rate him on the basis of what Attlee saw as his unstable political behaviour. Pre-empting a conversation, Attlee would cut Crossman dead: 'I saw your mother last week. She's looking very well' was an example of an Attlee put-down to a person whose behaviour fell short of what he believed acceptable. That wouldn't prevent Attlee, of course, asking how Crossman's parents were every time they met.

While being one of the Bevanite group organising a more radical alternative to Herbert Morrison's safety-first electoral approach, Crossman had been excluded from power. It was only the death of Hugh Gaitskell, in 1963, and the extraordinary rise of Harold Wilson, that offered Crossman an opportunity for his talents. The same was true of Barbara Castle.

Crossman had already used his position on the National Executive Committee of the Labour Party to help Labour rethink its welfare state strategy. From this power base, Crossman used his massive energy and talent to begin thinking anew what Beveridge should mean for the 1960s. He turned to Richard Titmuss, academic at the LSE, and to his followers, who were known as 'the Titmice', to help him. In some ways it was a wise choice for those wishing to revise Beveridge by striking down the main principle that underpinned Beveridge's reforms.

Titmuss, no doubt through the work of his fellow academic and assistant Tony Lynes, came up with superannuation proposals that broke with the flat rate contribution benefit levels then central to the Beveridge scheme. These new superannuation proposals were wage- and salary-related, both for contributions and benefits. Thus, the inequalities in work were taken forward into retirement; the price the Titmuss group believed had to be paid to gain widespread support for the necessary funding arrangements to any new scheme.

Crossman skilfully negotiated these proposals through the

National Executive Committee and through the Labour Party Conference, which was Labour's all-powerful sovereign decision-making body in those days. When Wilson came to power in 1964, he wisely brought Crossman and Castle into his government but, like so many prime ministers, didn't capitalise on the work these two figures had developed in opposition. They were, instead, both allocated to departments where they had to learn their new briefs. Crossman had the local government brief and was up against one of the great permanent secretaries of the day, Dame Evelyn Sharp.

He moved back to the social security brief a couple of years after Labour's landslide 1966 election win, when he was awarded the mammoth health and social security brief. He approached this task from his concrete tower at the Elephant and Castle with nothing but confidence. But confidence itself does not necessarily lead to political success.

The CPAG had been formed in 1965, both to draw attention to the numbers of poor children and their families, and to seek government remedy. When I joined CPAG in 1969 the poverty agenda was becalmed. The government had set up a range of inquiries after its 1964 election. Nothing followed from the series of reports that flooded on to ministers' desks in the run-up to what became the 1970 General Election. One has to doubt whether the intention was to receive the reports and then follow them with a programme of total inaction. Likewise on the CPAG front. When I arrived at the CPAG offices in 1969 the cupboard was bare of strategy or detailed policy proposals except for the beginnings of a memorandum that Tony Lynes had drafted. Tony was the first paid full-time secretary of the CPAG.

The memorandum would do nothing either to awaken the debate or, as I saw it, reposition CPAG as the premier independent poverty-lobbying organisation. I record elsewhere the chairman of CPAG, Peter Townsend's, unease at my suggestion of politicising the group manifesto by making it an attack on one of Labour's core 'myths'. I was also only too aware of my lack of knowledge of the poverty data.

When Peter first expressed his unease, I agreed to resign as the new head of CPAG if the strategy I was advocating to champion the poor and, at the same time, move the group from being seen as a mere appendage of the Labour Party to one of full independence as a lobby organisation, was unacceptable to the group. But I had warned Peter that CPAG was wasting away, and it would continue to wither unless it was reinvented. The campaign of 'The Poor Get Poorer Under Labour' was born from that memorandum I wrote.

I joined CPAG and had ringing in my ears a framework that Dick Crossman himself had used to teach students. It was in his reinterpretation of the classic 1867 study of the workings of the British constitution, by Walter Bagehot, that Crossman spelt out the power of political parties and their limitations. Parties were great mobilising forces, and their myths were crucial to their mobilising power over activists. A myth for Labour was its bias to the poor.

I initially believed the myth, but as I slowly built up my notebooks at CPAG I found that I couldn't square the myth with the reality of the government measures taken since 1964 – ones that I measured against protecting the poor. The reinvention of CPAG came from the document I drafted from material in those notebooks. Hence the memorandum's almost total repositioning of CPAG as an independent campaign for the poor that did not fear any government if it meant that the interests of the poor were at stake. I knew that blowing up Labour's central myth on its protection of the poor was political dynamite.

Peter Townsend and I were ushered into Crossman's room in the Cabinet Office. There before us was a polished table that looked the size of a football pitch. On Crossman's right was Brian Abel-Smith, along with Peter one of the central figures of the Titmice. He was much cleverer than Peter and had been the great innovator in health statistics and health policy ever since he joined the LSE from Cambridge.

Nothing could have prepared me for what followed. Crossman launched into Peter, attacking the document, shaking the document, shouting about the document and threatening him. How could we make such absurd claims that the poor were getting poorer under Labour?

Peter was sweating profusely and I witnessed Brian Abel-Smith sitting at his ring-side seat sniggering. It was an appalling sight for here were two friends who had done much to resurrect the poverty debate. The roaring continued. The table was banged. The one thing that Crossman didn't do was swing on the huge chandelier whose light fell on that extraordinarily well-polished table.

After three-quarters of an hour of this 'conversation' we left with Crossman roaring at us.

'What are you going to do with this?'

'We are going to publish it,' was my reply to Crossman's jeering. *The Times* already had a copy and we would see whether we were believed or not.

As we left, Brian Abel-Smith, in a snake-like manner, moved to our side and started talking to me about the tax threshold. I hadn't a clue about what he was muttering to me. In trying to draft the memorandum I discovered that no one on CPAG's executive committee could work out the clawback proposals that were central to the group's reform. I sensed we were in trouble. Since its first memorandum the group had proposed increasing family allowances (as cash benefit to families was then known) and clawing the increase back through child tax allowances from taxpayers who could reduce their tax liability by claiming their child tax allowances.

The group's weakness, of not understanding how the technicalities of its central reform operated, acted as a cover. What Abel-Smith was alerting us to, when muttering 'tax threshold, tax threshold...' out of the corner of his mouth, was that the point at which tax was being levied on income was below the tax threshold. Hence any increase in family allowances clawed back by adjusting child tax allowances would take the increase away from many families who were below what was beginning to be thought of as the official poverty line. But as the group did not understand the importance of this point, neither did almost anybody else in the country. Hence the political cover it gave to us while we sought both to understand and represent our position. We could argue that, at the very least, the increase would not be clawed back from *all* poor families. The full political effect of dramatic decline in the tax threshold in the post-war period would only be felt politically when the Tories used it, after their 1970 election win, to go back on their pre-election pledge to increase family allowances.

Here was a lesson for any lobbying group. No matter how smart your reform is, someone in the organisation does need to know how it might actually work out in practice. Abel-Smith's point was that the tax threshold was now below the supplementary benefit level. We would therefore be clawing back part of that increase from many of the working poor. It was shocking news to me, both to be told this and to hear it for the first time, given that the group was specialising in this wretched little reform that broke what I believed should be a universal provision of welfare.

Before Peter and I had moved to the Cabinet Office to see Crossman, I had given a pre-release document to *The Times*. *The Times* gave us a sizeable billing and from there other papers, including the *Guardian,* followed suit. We had opened the war in the media and we were winning against the government.

Unbeknownst to us, Crossman presented our paper to the Cabinet and reassured members that there was nothing in the document that should worry them. Such reassurance was given and accepted, even though the theme of 'The Poor Get Poorer Under Labour' was catching alight as if it were a bushfire in the Westminster village. It was being covered in the serious press and being raised in Parliament. But Crossman had answers to counter any points that could be raised.

That is until Roy Jenkins, the Chancellor of the Exchequer, broke tradition and discussed the outline of his 1969 budget with the whole Cabinet. Crossman made a bid for family allowance increases as being the most effective way of dealing with family poverty. But his slaughter of 'The Poor Get Poorer Under Labour' had been such that he persuaded the government that there was no need for action. Roy Jenkins reminded him of this and pushed him into the hole where Crossman had for a few months tried to bury Peter Townsend and me. In that hole Crossman remained, while we and everybody else were catapulted into a surprise 1970 election.

In the early 1970s, before Crossman was brought low by cancer, he came to a group AGM and was wonderfully thoughtful and kind to me. He asked whether I wanted a political career and I said yes. He encouraged me. But he did make the point that I had a very weak voice – I certainly had compared with him – and that I would find this a disadvantage. I always have.

# Keith Joseph

*'In a small way an action of mine played a rather*
*large part in Keith Joseph's political career.'*

For a decade from 1969 I edited *Poverty*, the quarterly journal of the CPAG. In 1978, I carried an article by Margaret and Arthur Wynn about the differential birth rate impact on Britain's social classes.

The article drew on birth data over time, showing that poorer families were out-birthing the rate among working and richer families. Sir Keith Joseph, as he was then called, in one of what would have been a series of speeches leading up to his bid to replace Edward Heath as Leader of the Opposition in 1970, spoke in terms that had more a hint of inter-war campaigns by the Eugenics Society.

Practically the whole of the press reacted as though Keith had emitted a great obscenity. It is a sign of how tightly, then as now, political correctness strangled any discussion of difficult social issues. Keith's response was typical and quick. A fulsome apology was linked to an act of self-imposed penance. He realised, he said, that he was 'unsuitable to run for the Tory leadership'. The article ran in CPAG's magazine and instead of opening up a great national debate, which has still to take place, it helped to enforce the restrictiveness on what is considered permissible public discussion. It also opened the way for Mrs T to try her luck in the Tory leadership stakes.

I had met Keith previously while he ruled the sprawling Department of Health and Social Security (DHSS) empire from the Goldfinger-designed tower at the Elephant and Castle in south London.

In the run-up to what turned out to be the 1970 election the Tories had publicly backed CPAG's call for an increase in what were then family allowances. I recall elsewhere the lead-up to CPAG's campaign on 'The Poor Get Poorer Under Labour'. I was keen on CPAG's increased status as an independent lobbying body, free of its association as a Labour Party appendage, but rather as a neutral organisation that simply offered support to anybody in power who dealt with the problems of destitution. This made me quite unpopular among the Labour ranks of course. And it marked the start of the group's rise to pre-eminence among the fast-growing field of social lobby organisation.

Despite our much-changed circumstances, access to a prime minister was not going to be that easy. One of my self-imposed tasks as CPAG's lobbyist was to read daily the Court Circular page in *The Times*. At that time it contained a mine of information on who mixed with who. The importance for me concerned the official dinners at Number 10. Who did Heath use to fill up the guest chairs, and what did this tell me about who he liked and trusted? Three women's names struck me: Diana Elles, Sara Morrison and Peggy Shepherd. I decided to take them in that order to see how sympathetic they were to our case and immediately found Diana Elles coming up trumps. Sara Morrison, as events were to teach me, was the closest to Heath of these three women, remaining an active and constant friend right to Heath's death. But Diana's enthusiasm was such that at this stage I did not trespass further into the ranks of the Tories good and great.

A meeting had been arranged to see Keith in his ministerial suite, which overlooked the Elephant and Castle roundabout and then further into South London. Diana accompanied me to lobby Keith on what the government's long-term plans were on the family income supplement and its now rebuffed sister of family benefit, family allowances.

Three things struck me as we were shown into Keith's office – its tidiness, its stunning panoramic view and a copy of Margaret Wynn's book *Family Policy* that was sitting on the right-hand side of an otherwise litter-free ministerial desk.

As we took our positions on the easy chairs placed past the desk and before the window I began the conversation with talking about the book. Keith waxed on the intellectual importance of Margaret's book – it was certainly affecting his thinking and that's not without currency, I thought. Then, in a guarded moment, he made a stereotypical comment about poor families.

Diana shot back and showed the value of those who combine book and personal knowledge. She explained that, as she was sure Keith knew, she had not only a role in the Tory hierarchy, but was also a voluntary school care worker 'just over there', as she pointed out of the window toward Walworth Road. 'We could go now, Keith, and you could meet families who know what you've said is wrong.' Keith immediately retreated and, as he offered an apology, the emphasis of his sorrow was matched by the appearance of deep furrows that quickly lined his forehead. We moved quickly to a discussion on Margaret's book.

I saw little of Keith when the Tories were returned to the

Opposition in 1974, but nothing of him when he became Industry and then Education Secretary in Mrs T's governments. I saw more of him after that when I gained sight of two lovable characteristics. One was his clearness and sharpness of mind. The other, his ability to laugh, not only at himself but gently at his colleagues.

We were standing on Westminster Underground station waiting for a District line train going westwards. It was after the Falklands Service in July 1982, and Robert Runcie's name came up. I made a defence of the archbishop who had been roughed up by parts of the media for his Falklands' sermon; it taught the need to pray for the families who were straddled on both sides, but who were united in grief at the loss of their loved ones in battle.

My criticism was different and aimed not at the archbishop's sermon, but that much of the music – which were works by Herbert Howe that I loved – should have been pieces that the congregation, representative of the nation, knew and could understand. To offer the diet that St Paul's did on that day was simply rude – one should never behave to guests in one's own house in a way that makes them feel uneasy. Keith listened patiently. Part of my defence was Robert's bravery. He had won the Military Cross in the Second World War for pulling some of his men free from a burning tank that could have exploded at any moment.

The District line train was now pulling into the station and I noticed that, when Keith was about to deliver what he thought was a knockout blow, his lips made a pronounced effort in throwing forth the words. His look took on an extra crafting role as he said there was all the difference between physical and moral courage. I began as quickly as I could to reel off the names of people I knew who were brave physically and not morally, and vice versa. Keith remained very gentle with me.

Much later, when Keith was in the Lords, he would take me to tea in their rich, somewhat overdone Pugin dining-room. As you go through the main entrance into this long L-shaped room, on the left there is a dining-room for the exclusive use of their Lordships. To the right, in another L-shaped room, is a bevy of tables of different sizes to which their Lordships can invite guests.

The rule then in the Peers' Dining Room was that, as peers come in for their lunch or dinner, they should occupy the first vacant seat at either side of the long table that dominates the room. Such a rule, with Parliament having more than its fair share of bores, was invented either by the kindest of souls, or one who wished to randomly and regularly inflict the pain of boredom on his colleagues.

Keith invariably took me to a table for two where he would act as mother by pouring the tea and ensuring that I ate my toasted tea cake. These teas, and the snatched conversation we would have as we met walking toward our various business around the Palace of Westminster, were a revelation. Keith would bring to our tea dates his current reading list and challenge me as to whether I had read the set text drawn from the most important books – in his view – that he had with him or was reading.

On one occasion, he had the volume written by Charles Murrey who was to become a major contributor, and for a time the leader, of the debate on whether or not Britain had an underclass. We followed the set procedure. Had I read the Murrey book that he handed over the table? God, I thought. I was just completing writing a book on the same topic and had provisionally given it the same title, *Losing Ground*. I was winded and, far from battling with Keith, I kept thinking about what title I might give to my volume. By the end of tea, I had renamed it, *Losing Out*.

What became apparent from these tea parties, and our snatched conversations from around the Palace as our paths crossed, were the clear insightful views Keith had about his colleagues. Behind that mad monk exterior, as the media loved to dub him, was a highly critical and evaluative mind. His comments sometimes shocked me, as it was obvious that he was only too well aware of how duplicitous some of his colleagues could be and how others would undertake acts of extraordinary kindness.

But Keith's humour was dominant. The smallest comment could get us laughing. And we laughed often at the silliest side of life, laughter that would reach a climax as he fought for more breath to keep his laughter going, and I would have tears streaming down my face. He cared little for the strange looks invariably cast our way by his colleagues as both of us panted for breath. Such confidence I suppose, in part, came from being part of the Joseph family.

# Mark Bonham Carter

*'His attraction was like a spell over me*
*whenever I was near his company.'*

It was the Runcimans who first introduced me to Mark Bonham
Carter, as they did to so many of their friends. On the same day
that I would unknowingly meet Mark, I had read his review of the
first volume of *The Crossman Diaries*. As I was to learn, the brilliance
of the review was characteristic of all Mark's writings. I had written
him a postcard and put it in my pocket with the intention of posting
it on my way to the Runciman party.

I am normally terrified of arriving at parties and sometimes feign
illness, or induce an illness upon myself, so that I don't actually ring
the doorbell, such is my nervousness. But on this occasion, for some

reason, I was not at all consumed by fear or nerves. I could have been, given the size of the Runcimans' house. The door swung open and I was greeted with the legendary W.G. Runciman smile. Any fears were forgotten and in I went to the party.

Mark became more and more interested and agitated as we spoke. I replied as best I could, but as the evening progressed Mark, whose back was resting against the wall, slowly descended so we were both sitting on the floor. I had the most wonderful evening and on my way home I realised the postcard remained unposted. It was sent to Mark. The Runcimans thought Mark had behaved in an aggressive manner toward me, but I thought nothing of the kind; my only regret was that I hadn't personally given him my card. Mark was awfully stricken once he received the postcard. I only learned this much later in life. What was immediate was that the postcard acted as a messenger for a much-wanted friendship.

Mark responded with his characteristic generosity, and a life-long friendship was forged.

From that day, there was no major political move, or book that I wished to publish, upon which I didn't consult Mark. He always made time available to me, and greatly improved whatever I was proposing. And so, as they say, it came to pass, after the leak to the press about child benefit. I had never been particularly interested in reforming the Official Secrets Act, seeing as how it plays a necessary part in public safety. But I did feel a responsibility to 'Deep Throat'[1] and was anxious that yet another idea being picked up from America had led to a Freedom of Information Bill.

At this time Mark was working at the Outer Circle Policy Unit. 'Yes,' he said, 'We will undertake the seminars in preparation for the bill.' And then I learned another important aspect of alcohol's beneficial role in politics. Toward the end of our work, Mark took the

---

1. 'Deep Throat' refers to the secret informant who, in 1972, provided key details to the media in the U.S. Watergate scandal.

whole working party group off to a country house. The actual time spent on the bill, I thought, was pathetically small, and the amount of time to drink was exorbitantly large. But it was during these long alcoholic breaks that much of the breakthrough and many of the bill's improvements were secured. Mark presided over us like a wise raven, pecking here, pecking there, pecking everywhere to ensure we left with a workable paper.

This was the bill that Clement Freud then introduced to the House of Commons. So began the official movement of having a bill to reform the Official Secrets Act.

One of the kindnesses Mark and Leslie showed me was an invitation to Leslie's house toward the toe of Italy. The site had been chosen by her mother and a better place couldn't have been found; but I was not with them on Mark's last trip in 1994. It was one of his favourite places for holidaying. I learned later what had happened. Mark and his daughter Jane had been climbing a local mountain. Mark always had a really good eye for women. He pointed out to Jane the beauty of one creature who was some distance from them, then, within seconds, he suffered a heart attack and died. In some ways, for him perhaps, what a marvellous way it was to go; but Leslie and her family and his huge circle of friends were naturally bereft. No more the drinking, no more the humour, no more the extraordinary amount of smoking and no more the high intelligence. My political life would have been so different had I had Mark to talk to while I was a minister. He would have patiently explained how I was being sewn up by the Brown axis and what I should be doing about it; but there was no Mark, and so no long career in politics for me. But that's only a small loss. Mark had the same ability as John Vaizey if you saw him at a party. He would the centre of fun, laughter and mirth – a centre to which people were invariably attracted. It was not only at parties that I was charmed by Mark. His attraction was like a spell over me whenever I was near his company.

# Edward Heath

*'Yes. Yes. No. Yes. Yes – if it's to our advantage. Waldegrave… tea!'*

Edward Heath was replying to the questions I had posed arising from a pre-Budget report that the CPAG had submitted to the Chancellor; we had sent to Heath as Leader of the Opposition in 1968.

We were meeting him in the Leader of the Opposition's office looking directly over the Thames. We had moved through a tiny office staffed by a couple of secretaries and William Waldegrave, who I assumed was Heath's Chief of Staff. Today the Leader of the Opposition employs up to twenty members of parliamentary staff and this huge change in numbers has had two profound political effects.

The first is the relationship between the leader and his party HQ. With such a tiny staff in the Commons, there was no taxpayers' grant, or 'Short Money'[1] as it is now called, for the Opposition parties. The Leader of the Opposition was therefore much more dependent on his own wit and abilities, and for backup from the small numbers of researchers in the various party headquarters. This, and dependence on the party HQ being a place of researching policy, is now almost non-existent. The PR role instead reigns supreme.

The second change concerns the power of staff in the Leader of the Opposition's office, whose numbers have swelled way beyond what is necessary for an intelligent Leader of the Opposition. Funding for Opposition parties, or Short Money, has become additionally paramount due to increased opposition representation, media influence in politics, and the rising costs of parliamentary work. It aims to level the playing field, to ensure effective scrutiny of the government. Money, and the staff it provides, have taken over the function of the Leader of the Opposition's brain.

It took Heath, I suppose, a full forty-five seconds to answer the twelve or so questions I posed to him. I would have been quite happy to have concluded the meeting there and then and left. We had gained all the knowledge we required, when the Opposition would apply pressure, when it would or would not, depending on the day and the movement in current debate. But no. Heath, surprisingly given the press he received about his curtness, had an idea of the decencies and rhythms of public life, or at least that was what I concluded. Meetings that were serious would take a certain period of time, hence his call to William Waldegrave for tea. Tea was indeed produced, and forty-four minutes and fifteen seconds of awkward conversation followed.

Throughout that conversation Heath talked exclusively about

---

1. Named after Edward Short who first proposed funding for opposition parties. It was first paid in 1975.

sailing – even down to the minutiae – explaining the reactions of people on land who would wave to him as he skippered his yacht *Morning Cloud*. Why, he pondered aloud, did people wave when he could hardly see and certainly not recognise who they were? Perhaps, I wondered, people were fonder of him than he ever thought possible, and they were certainly impressed by his sailing prowess. What other Leader of the Opposition has achieved the equivalent of winning the Sydney to Hobart race, one of the world's toughest ocean races?

I only had one further meeting with Heath, much later when he was a backbencher. Eleanor Rathbone (1872–1946)[2] was to me the most impressive backbench Member of Parliament since William Wilberforce in the early nineteenth century. Yet, the House of Commons had no memorial to her. Eleanor, social reformer and independent MP, had allowed few portraits to be painted, although a fine one by Sir James Gunn used to hang in the National Portrait Gallery. Its fate is a salutary lesson on how this nation is all too often programmed to wipe out its own collective memory.

In a reassessment of twentieth-century exhibits, the National Portrait Gallery committed Eleanor's portrait to the dungeons, where other unwanted and forgotten heroes are stored. What fate can there be for a nation that is so cavalier with its memories of greatness? I subsequently wrote to the National Portrait Gallery enquiring why they hadn't found room for her. At the time they were not interested. Her portrait by Sir James Gunn now hangs on the second floor of the gallery.

Eleanor after all was not only a major figure in what I would call the second wave of suffragettes, but she was distinguished on so many

---

2. In 1919 Rathbone was elected president of the National Union of Societies for Equal Citizenship (formerly the National Union of Women's Suffrage Societies). She was prominent in abolishing Liverpool's slums and fighting to improve education, wages and working hours.

fronts. I would place her important 1924 report *The Disinherited Family* alongside Beveridge's great volume on full employment, making, as it does, a plea for greater equality of income within and between families.

But her connection with Heath lay in appeasement; and her record at beating Churchill in drawing attention to the evils of Hitler and the folly of appeasing his demands.

For Heath, too, had a most admirable record against appeasement, even though then he was an Oxford undergraduate and not, like Eleanor, a major public figure. But in a phrase coined about him by one of his small number of staff: actions speak louder than words. He was an active campaigner against the Chamberlain government's policy of endlessly appeasing Hitler. He fought, in my eyes, on the right side of the great 1938 Oxford by-election, when the Master of Balliol, A.D. Lindsay, opposed the appeasement candidature of Quintin Hogg (later Lord Hailsham). Despite this, just two years later, Hogg voted against Chamberlain in The Norway Debate after the failed Norwegian Campaign against Nazi Germany, leading to Chamberlain's resignation and paving the way for Churchill to assume office as Prime Minister during the Second World War.

I guess therefore that Heath would have a soft spot for Eleanor and so it proved. How could it be that the House of Commons had no portrait of one of its greatest and most distinguished members? I sought out Betty Boothroyd (then an MP) to support a campaign for a likeness to be made of the Gunn portrait; I wanted her and Heath to lead this.

Betty enthusiastically agreed and so I sought a meeting with Heath. The day arrived and either I was early or he was slightly late. He came into his House of Commons rooms (a far more spacious office than the one he occupied as Leader of the Opposition when planning for government). Down he fell in his big chair. I had written to him beforehand outlining how I hoped he would co-lead the restitution of the Rathbone portrait, so before I uttered a word he yelled, 'Yes. Of course I will.' And that was that.

'Wow!' I exclaimed. As we become older, as a general rule, we tend to take more time possibly recollecting events that may or may not be relevant before arriving at the point of discussion.

'My first meeting with you, Ted, could have been over in forty-five seconds. This one's been completed in five. Thank-you.'

And I left, armed with his support and with his shoulder humping up and down in total merriment at the thought.

# Michael Foot

I followed up the letter I wrote to Michael Foot before the Whitsun Recess by calling into his room. It was 9 June 1980. He began by thanking me again for writing and was clearly chuffed about the students' views.

But he was rather vague about what his intentions were. I said it was almost inevitable that we would have a leadership contest after the Party Conference. Eric Heffer had stated his intention to stand and I expressed the view that many of us would find it impossible to support Eric; we would therefore need other candidates to come into the ring.

Michael seemed genuinely humble about his own role, and intimated that he was too old. 'It might well be so,' I said, 'but you are the best person to stop Denis Healey.' His view was that Denis would tear the party apart, and that he did wish to prevent Denis being successful in the leadership contest. My view was more that he would *boot* it apart, and Michael agreed this was probably a more accurate description of what would happen.

Michael was much more sensitive than I with the mechanics of this conflict. He saw a Healey leadership as one that will increase tensions between the Parliamentary Labour Party and the National Executive Council. He explained his sympathies were largely on the side of the PLP, but clearly didn't want to exaggerate differences or needlessly rough up members of the NEC. This bridge building was one of his great strengths at that time.

I suggested that as the leadership obviously came up in conversation from time to time, could I perhaps say something about his intentions. He agreed: I could feed back that he had 'not ruled out the possibility' of standing in an autumn leadership election.

Next I asked about the newspaper coverage of his support for Peter Shore. He was generous about Shore to the nth degree; said he was radical and effective in Cabinet, and much more so than many people who were now trying to grab the headlines. He clearly didn't rate Wedgewood-Benn very highly, and went on to say that one day Peter Shore would make a fine leader of the Labour Party. I carefully expressed no comment, but did say that I thought it inconceivable that Shore could win an election that year. Michael agreed, so I drove home my view that Michael's strength meant he would take some MPs' votes who would, in his absence, vote for Healey. He accepted this point.

I remember feeling that if we did face an autumn leadership contest we may need the goodwill of Shore voters in the later ballots, so I asked Michael whether I could therefore talk to Jack Straw and report his long-term support for Shore. He agreed.

At no point during our conversation did Michael suggest that anybody else had offered to play the necessary role of broker. Last time round it was Neil Kinnock, and I wondered why he was not offering his services again? In addition, one scenario that might keep Callaghan in the contest this autumn was not discussed at our meeting. We had both agreed that, other things being equal, a contest this autumn would not include Callaghan as a candidate: but if the Party Conference overthrew all or most of the constitutional changes proposed and agreed last year, things could change. In these circumstances, and with the possibility of a Healey win, this could significantly increase the chances of the party being torn apart. Hence my feeling that Callaghan would 'allow' himself to be drafted.

A last point: I noticed how Michael expressed no personal animosity to other candidates. Indeed, he went out of his way to say he was on good terms with Denis but simply thought him the wrong candidate at this time.

# Enoch Powell

*Enoch enquired about my response to his lectures.*
*'You're opening yourself up to a heresy trial', I replied.*
*'Could you arrange such a trial, for that will ensure*
*my safe return in South Down?'*

Important business can take place in the House of Commons'
lavatories. For one thing, you never know if you are being
overheard or, more importantly, not being overheard. And likewise,
it is difficult to immediately rush away. Conversation can be a good
alternative to standing in there silently.

The pact, if that is not too strong a word, between Enoch Powell
and Harold Wilson, was forged in the Aye Lobby's loo in the House
of Commons. When votes are called, members file into either the

Aye Lobby – to vote for a motion – or into the No Lobby that runs alongside the other side of the Chamber, this time on the Speaker's left. As members are locked in the lobbies for a short period of time, the House authorities thought it sensible to provide lavatories.

It was Enoch's chance encounter with Harold Wilson in the Aye Lobby loo that provided him with the chance to let Harold know that during the following weekend he, Enoch, was to make a major speech telling voters to vote Labour in the general election should they desire the opportunity to vote on a European Economic Community renegotiation.

My own conversation with Enoch was in another lavatory – the one situated off the library corridor. It was much less momentous in terms of the politics of the nation but it led to a reserved friendship with Enoch – reserved, I add, on Enoch's side. I never met any MP who managed to get through this wall of reserve.

Enoch had been giving a series of lectures at Zion College – then an outstanding library for London clergy – that were picketed by Christians who had been styled radical by the media. I apologised to Enoch for not being at the gatherings and he immediately asked if I would like to read his lectures.

'I would,' was my reply.

'They will be on the board within an hour.'

The board, as it is called, is a place where letters, committee papers and small packets can be left for an MP to collect. A copy of the three lectures were on the board well within the hour, together with a beautifully written note forged by a dip-in ink pen and expressing interest to hear my response.

I was ready with my answer soon afterwards. MPs were trapped in the Commons on one of what I found intolerable all-night, or near-all-night, sittings. These sittings gave me some sense, as a new member, of eternal hell fire, or at least a condition of work that brought me pretty near to the fire. Enoch, in contrast, gave every appearance of loving these events; here was the legislature holding the executive to account. That was one, if not the greatest, function of the House of Commons for Enoch.

Here was a major difference between us on how power was exercised through the British constitution. Bagehot noted how power had moved from the monarch to the Lords and to the Commons in the mid-nineteenth century. Power had moved on again since then and the Commons, I believe, retains only the duties Bagehot apportioned to the monarch: the right to be consulted, to advise and to warn. Power now lies with that small coterie or gang who gather around the prime minister of the day.

Enoch was forever wishing the Commons to re-establish its past sovereignty over the executive and keeping the government up all night, if need be, was one means of doing so. I saw the matter differently. As soon as I entered, the Commons was for me the formal setting within which the constitution ensured an election campaign would take place every five years. It had other functions, of course. A vote can be a very effective warning system to individual ministers about their programme, as much as it can be to a government. But fighting a five-year election campaign was now our major role almost day in day out. One party would try to impress a favourable image of themselves in the voters' minds, and, conversely, pin an unfavourable image on their opponents. This new role seems to fit our adversarial system.

The lectures excited me, and I longed to discuss them with their author. I went looking for him, yet Enoch was not in his usual place in the library, writing his beautiful handwritten letters or speeches with one of the library's dip-in, steel-nibbed pens. Nor did I catch him at the early morning votes where records showed that he had voted. Our paths finally crossed in what Enoch would have regarded as the same day (as Parliament had sat right through the night), but those of us who had gone home to bed after the 2 a.m. vote thought of as a new dawn.

He enquired what I thought of his lectures. 'You are opening yourself up for a heresy trial,' I replied, for this beautifully written text argued either that Jesus was stoned to death, or that the key New Testament figure was actually John the Baptist. I cannot for the life of me now recall which, but the proposition would have been beautifully constructed, despite being built on what I felt were the shakiest of foundations.

Enoch laughed. 'Could you arrange such a heresy trial, for that would ensure my safe return in South Down? A trial will enhance my return.' Sadly, I failed to gain him his heresy trial and defeat awaited him in 1987 at the next election.

A lasting impression of Enoch was on an all too different plane of activity. My mother and I were walking into Westminster Abbey one Sunday morning. Coming from a different angle toward the West Door were Enoch and his wife, Pam. They were a little ahead and Enoch passed through into the Abbey without any acknowledgement, let alone breaking those ever so stiff facial muscles into the hint of a smile.

It proved more difficult for Enoch to avoid me as we left. 'Why are you ignoring us?' I enquired.

Enoch's eyes fell upon me. 'I had no wish to embarrass you by presuming our acquaintance in front of a person to whom I had not had the privilege of being introduced.'

Laughter from me, my mother, and Pam greeted this extraordinary statement.

'Enoch!' exclaimed Pam. And with that we entered a taxi and sped toward their home in South Eaton Place. There was much merriment and some drink, with me becoming, as my mother commented later, squiffy.

On our way home, my mother commented what a wonderful morning she had had.

'Meeting Enoch?' I asked.

'No, you silly boy,' she firmly replied. 'It was going to the Abbey for the Holy Mysteries, and *then* to encounter the mystery of Enoch and his so lovable Pam.' That was her stunning summary of our morning adventure. Both mysteries endure.

# Robert Runcie

*'How do you intend to mould the bench of bishops?'*
*'Why do you ask that?'*
*'During your stewardship you will appoint*
*over half of the House of Bishops.'*
*'How did you find that out?'*
*'I checked the age of all those who are currently bishops*
*against the date at which they will compulsory retire.'*

The Archbishop of Canterbury, Robert Runcie, had invited me to tea in the House of Lords. Here I was sitting alongside the great man himself. We shared toasted teacakes swimming in butter, and downed what the waiter euphemistically called 'workman's tea'.

I pressed Robert for the kind of qualities he would look for in appointing to the bench. There was no clear answer. He looked puzzled. Surely someone holding a top job had a clear idea of the three or four major goals they wanted to achieve during their allotted time span. In the case of the Archbishop of Canterbury, here was someone who could enjoy the benefit of appointing half the generals who would help deliver his strategy.

I could not decide then or since whether this was because Robert had given no conscious effort in thinking through who would fill these key posts, or if he preferred not to describe the type of person he was looking for. I could not help thinking of this supposed absence of strategy when I read what became the infamous, anonymous, Crockford's Preface,[1] written by the priest Gareth Bennett and published in December 1987, which lambasted poor old Runcie and accused him of all sorts of failings, centring around his alleged failure to lead. It was the discovery of Garry Bennett's authorship of this waspish piece that led to Bennett's suicide a few days after the publication. In this long charge sheet against Robert, one of Bennett's arguments was that the Archbishop chose for promotion from a limited pool of talent, and in doing so he excluded the Catholic wing of the Anglican Church of which Bennett was a most prominent member.

Bennett was also talented. He would help draft some of Robert's addresses. Although not perhaps the greatest of Church historians, such as Norman Sykes, he was the best the Church could boast of at that time – itself a somewhat chilling illustration of the decline of Anglicanism in our common culture.

Bennett had taken me up, possibly after hearing of my friendship with Mrs T and her proactive policy in appointing Deans, Regius professorships and a willingness to break the convention that prime ministers would choose the first of any two names submitted to

---

1. A forty-page preface to *Crockford's Clerical Directory* that was published anonymously but later revealed as written by the Reverend Dr Gareth Bennett, Oxford Don and Anglican priest (1929–1987).

them in appointing a vacant bishopric. His intelligence did not fail him here as Mrs T was always open to names for these posts – and sometimes beyond into secular appointments which were in her gift or influence. I had lobbied for Bennett to be given a deanery but Mrs T was resolutely unforthcoming, her face remaining totally still when his name came up. What, I wondered, had the old informal network said of Bennett?

At our tea Robert was sitting there, his purple bishop's bib looking of an expensive kind, shining, with the silky weave clearly visible. Above lay that fractured face showing all too well the trouble and travail of this world. Crowning that face was a block of hair that gave, on one side, every appearance of being waved in a way that was so fashionable in the 1950s. His reed-like voice and face spoke only of kindness, but kindness alone does not see a candidate onto St Augustine's throne and the premier position in the worldwide Anglican Communion. What else was there, I wondered?

But this meeting was long before the Bennett affair, and Robert had no doubt asked me to tea to weigh me up. He was to nominate me to Synod where I naturally joined what I thought to be Robert's wing of Church politics. They may have labelled themselves Catholic but within this grouping was more than a fair share who seemed possessed by a hard, unbending puritanism when it came to the crucial business of give and take in Church politics.

The issue that consumed attention was that of appointing women priests. I had been a convert to the cause ever since spending a summer in America soon after becoming an MP. A scholarship had been awarded by the American Embassy and I joked to the American Ambassador that it was obviously CIA-inspired. 'Why shouldn't the CIA do something good for America?' I enquired of a somewhat shocked ambassador.

At this time I had doubts on how best to establish the priesthood among women. Should we make the reform in step with other parts of the Catholic Church, or break ranks and go for it ourselves? I tended to be part of the cautious lobby.

Such were my thoughts on my trip as I searched for a sacred space in Washington and found it in the Victorian pile that is Washington Cathedral. I have enjoyed, since childhood, a remarkable Alice-like ability to fall down any hole that presents itself. Washington Cathedral proved to be no exception to this rule. Walking about admiring the sheer height of the building I passed an entrance to the crypt. And, like Alice, I began a great fall. Down the steps I tumbled running ever faster in an attempt to maintain my balance.

The end of the hole came into view. But I was falling so fast I couldn't slow my speed as I hit the highly polished marble floor. Out I glided to what I could see was an altar. And not only an altar, but an altar in use. An unsuspecting priest was celebrating the holy mysteries as I slid toward the altar. My eyes turned to the right and beheld the members of the congregation, not all of whom were now focused on the greatness of the mysteries as another mystery slid toward the celebrant.

I came to halt on the south side and remained there as if the position had been pre-ordained. My embarrassment ceased as I began to engage in what was before me. Now I saw that it was a woman priest and, as the mysteries continued, one in particular unfolded to me. Could there be anything more natural than a woman priest? My Pauline conversion was complete.

But while I totally supported Robert's open-minded position on women priests, I disagreed with him on what became known as the 'bag of bones' politics. This was a comment the Bishop of Durham, David Jenkins, had made about the Resurrection.[2] Jenkins struck me as a kindly but essentially daft fool, although not beyond pouring

---

2. Bishop Jenkins, when talking about the resurrection on Radio 4 (1984, *Poles Apart*), had referred to the Resurrection by saying: 'After all, a conjuring trick with bones only proves that it is as clever as a conjuring trick with bones.'

shafts of light on some issues.

Synod was consumed by angst, and not a little fury, over Jenkin's comments. A motion was debated on how the hierarchy should respond. I spoke in this debate and made what must have been my most appalling contribution anywhere.

It was not terrible in the sense of speaking badly. My wretched contribution was probably one of the better delivered efforts that day. Synod, like the House of Commons, was always quiet, almost reverential, when I spoke, and it was so when I contributed to the debate on the Bishop of Durham's 'heresy'.

During that speech I uttered a phrase, the immediate consequence of which has haunted me ever since. Addressing the assembled company, I sought an escape for the archbishop. I pleaded that he should not respond now but go away after the debate and consider what Durham had said – then, when times were quieter, come back to Synod. Totally reasonable and helpful. But then I added a further phrase.

Harry Cust was an indescribably colourful and witty Conservative MP who had sat in the Commons from 1890 to 1895 for a Lincolnshire constituency, then for Bermondsey from 1900 to 1906. He was reputed by some to be Lady Diana Cooper's father, and I often wondered jokingly if he hadn't played a similar role with Mrs Thatcher's advent into the world. Mr Cust was known as one of the great philanderers of his day.

Cust was present in the House during one of those interminable debates on tariff reform in which Prime Minister Balfour took part. Balfour was the very clever but sometimes defeatist leader who didn't dare articulate his mind on tariff reform for fear of irreconcilably splitting his party into two clear warring factions. Cust mocked the Prime Minister, and firmly nailed his colours to the fence as he always did.

I ended my contribution to the Durham debate with suggesting Robert Runcie escape today's debate by taking away what we had said for further thought. But I added a hope that, when he returned, he would be more decisive on this issue. It was a phrase that Bennett quoted, inaccurately, in the main charge against Robert in his anonymous attack in Crockford's Preface.

Robert had made it a political act not to nail his colours to the fence, although it was a stance that deeply annoyed both extremes in Church politics. The Synod rocked with laughter as I thought it would, but Robert looked over to me with such hurt – the kind of look Judas would have received as his identifying kiss landed on to his master's cheek.

I curl as I recall this cheap, successful move, which stabbed at the heart of Robert's kindness and, equally importantly, his political strategy. He knew, as I was to learn, that the Church of England had now become ungovernable. Nailing one's colours to the fence probably felt the only strategy to keep its body and soul together. And in that art Robert Runcie was the twentieth century's supreme exemplar.

# Margaret Thatcher

*'Shall I follow you, Prime Minister?'*
*'People usually do.'*

I met Mrs T, as I still think of her, on a number of occasions when she was Prime Minister to lobby on behalf of my constituents and on public appointments. As soon as I was elected as an MP in 1979, trade union leaders in the local Cammell Laird shipyard asked me to lobby the Prime Minister for Navy orders, and so I established a cross-party group to do so, inviting those Merseyside MPs who wished to join me. The old Labour guard was hostile but with that trade union request, I had cover, no matter how much the so-called far left grumbled about my actions.

Access was relatively easy until way into Mrs T's stewardship;

I had rarely been excluded from access. Now, toward the end of her premiership, requests for a meeting with the PM simply went unanswered. I warned her bag carrier, Archie Hamilton – the MP billed as her Private Parliamentary Secretary – that if he kept the portcullis down I would kidnap her, and tell her that it was not only was I being excluded from the court, but so too, and crucially important to her future, were a range of views of certain backbenchers whose opinions sat to the right of Genghis Khan's.

That evening I had been invited to a dinner at The Dorchester Hotel on Park Lane to discuss a topic I no longer recall. Des Wilson, who had been a premier social lobbyist while at Shelter, was speaking about God knows what. Boredom had driven me to drink, but it was a pleasant journey. I was distinctly squiffy, to use the phrase so often attributed to the consequences of Asquith's alcoholic consumption, by the time I arrived back at the House for the 10 p.m. vote.

And there, on the MPs' letterboard in our lobby, was a note informing me that the portcullis was being raised. The Prime Minister would see me immediately after we voted. 'God,' I tried to think, 'what was it that I wanted to lobby her on?'

My mind remained befuddled as I made my way after voting to the other lobby where the Tory MPs were emerging. Unlike the prime ministers who followed after Mrs T – Blair, Brown and Cameron – Mrs T missed few votes and was invariably one of the last to be counted out. She remained as long as possible to allow her own side to lobby her.

At last, the Prime Minister swept by, and I called after her, 'Shall I follow you, Prime Minister?' 'People usually do,' came her swift reply. I longed to have had a mirror in front of the PM's face. Surely a hint of a smile would have registered. As instructed, I duly followed her along the corridor and into the Prime Minister's Room behind the Speaker's Chair; along that same corridor where prime ministers and chancellors have had their parliamentary base ever since Pugin and

Barry so spectacularly rebuilt the House of Commons after the Great Fire of 1834.

The room is L-shaped with the larger part facing the room's entrance and hosting a Cabinet table for official meetings. To the right was a more than decent-sized alcove with two sofas, an armchair and a television set. Mrs T was reported to be able to drink anyone under the table.

'What will you have to drink?' was delivered more as a ministerial instruction than a question.

'What is there?' I asked.

'Whisky,' came the reply.

'May I please have a very, *very* weak whisky please?'

'I, too, will have a very, *very* weak whisky,' chimed the Prime Minister with an all too recognisable take-off of my voice.

So, despite all protestations to the contrary it appeared that this old girl did have more than a slight sense of humour. Here was the second time in one evening when she had gently sent me up.

I pondered what to do with the unwanted glass of alcohol. I wasn't the first and can't believe I'll be the last victim to be invited to drink in the PM's study when drink is the last thing the invitee wanted. Rab Butler, when faced with an equally determined prime minister, Churchill, poured his unwanted whisky into his shoe. But Churchill was sloshed. Mrs T was far from that state of grace, and she remained as eagle-eyed as ever.

The drinks appeared. One was almost black. The other coloured like gentle hay. Mrs T's hand swept over the tray and bagged what looked like neat whisky. I gratefully received the soda-watered one; then the lobbying business began.

I had been a lobbyist for CPAG in the olden days, when lobbying had yet to emerge fully from the Garden of Eden. Once in the House, my old training immediately came into play. Who would give up the possibility of lobbying the most powerful person in the country?

So, the nature of tonight's business was fired as a question from the steely-eyed Prime Minister, but I still for the life of me couldn't think what the hell I wanted to lobby her on. I hit on ecclesiastical appointments. I mentioned that a particular deanery was vacant and asked if she would consider a certain name.

She hesitated and remained uncharacteristically vague in her response, which struck me as unusual.

'Is it because he is unmarried, Prime Minister?' I asked. (The candidate was in a partnership with another man.) 'Shouldn't we reward faithfulness, not promiscuity?'

'O-oh, f..a..i..t..h..f..u..l..n..e..s..s, of course,' came her reply. But still she resisted my nomination.

Within the month, a scandal had engulfed my candidate. Yet on other appointments, such as a Regius Professor of History, she was resolute and acted quickly. 'You have your candidate,' I was informed on one occasion, bringing the meeting to an end.

Of course, meetings with someone who was so clearly shaping our history both excited and fascinated me. But she was different from every subsequent prime minister. Nothing in her record suggested she would become one of the three great prime ministers of the twentieth century. Her record as Education Secretary was pretty pedestrian. But somehow the fairies that circled around her cot had bestowed on her the quality of driving a programme – her programme – through the civil service machine, in a way that came to evoke more than a mini social and economic revolution.

The power to decide and drive through decisions appealed to me. And this power was never better displayed than during my second to last meeting with Mrs T before she resigned. I had subsequent meetings, including one on the night she was deciding whether or not to resign, but by then the power position between us had changed, as I will later describe. I was no longer coming to ask Big Mama to help me in my chosen task. But that is the approach I followed with the

Lady and, if she engaged, she never failed to deliver.

This meeting was at the close of the day Mrs T had flown back from the US after 'putting some backbone into President Bush', as she kept stressing to me. George Bush, of course, became President Bush Snr once his son was elected to the same office. This was the only meeting I attended in her study at Number 10. She was as high as a kite, excited beyond belief.

'You don't realise that I had to put backbone into him to fight the war,' she triumphantly asserted, as she marched around and around her study.

The 'you've no *idea*...' was occasionally interrupted by my protestations for her to sit down and talk with me. I was anxious to get her agreement on a Navy order for Cammell Laird.

'*You've* no idea...' continued the Prime Minister, as yet again I tried to interrupt her thoughts, or at least her words. Finally, and perhaps momentarily tired of recalling her day of triumph, she sat down smartly beside me.

'What do you want?' came a clearly puzzled voice, as if witnessing a key page of history being turned was not enough.

I made my bid for an order.

'Is that *all* you want?' yelped the Prime Minister before jumping up and reprising the 'you've *no* idea...' refrain. I retreated, pleased by her commitment, but simply bowled over by being privy to this extraordinary scene in which Mrs T played out her thinking and rightly took satisfaction in having persuaded the Americans to be bold.

Wirral then returned four MPs. Three were Tories, two were members of the government, and I was the single Labour member. The Tories, therefore, had more opportunities than I did for lobbying behind the scenes. For our lobby to be effective, each of us needed to keep the others informed as we went about our business, particularly concerning efforts to win Navy orders for our yard.

However, on this occasion, I was so elated by what the PM had disclosed in our meeting that I remained on cloud nine throughout the next day and completely neglected my secretarial duties to my fellow MP lobbyists. I hadn't written to the Wirral Tory MPs who formed a crucial part in lobbying for Cammell Laird orders. Then, on the third day, so to speak, I was brought back firmly to earth.

Walking through the wonderfully designed Barry corridor that now links Portcullis House to the House of Commons I saw David Hunt, approaching from the other direction. David was one of Wirral's four lobbyists and a Tory member. *Oh God,* I thought, *I've not told him about my prime ministerial meeting.*

Hesitantly, and stuttering somewhat, I began to apologise.

'No apology needed,' came his swift reply. 'The relevant Secretaries of State and Permanent Secretaries have received a PM's minute detailing your conversation and the conclusion. Congratulations!' was David's graceful response, although he could barely control his laughter.

This was what I so admired about her. Mrs T had helped sway an ally to expel Saddam Hussein from Kuwait. I had never seen her as excited as she was that night, knowing that she had rolled the dice across the board, and to her advantage. No one had been present at our meeting – no one ever was – but, excited or not, she had dictated her minutes recording the decisions of our meeting to a secretary she must have had to search for. Only then, I imagine, would she have gone off to find another audience to listen to her 'putting backbone into the man' refrain that had so mesmerised me.

In November 1990, Chris Patten and I had been invited to The Travellers Club to meet senior members of the Pilgrim Trust. Time went by and there was no sign of Chris. It was the evening Mrs T had to decide whether to fight on or resign. Hugely late, the doors opened and there was Chris, smarming down his hair while muttering that today was the worst day of his life.

He had been to see her, like all Cabinet members, who she had invited into a meeting individual by individual. He reported to the whole room that he had told Mrs T that her time was up.

On the way back, in his ministerial car, I asked Chris whether he had actually said what he reported to the meeting of astonished Pilgrim trustees; he replied he hadn't. For reasons that are still unknown to me, I announced that I would see her – and tell her that time was up.

Chris thought this a good idea and dropped me at the Members' Entrance to the House of Commons from where I made my way immediately to the Prime Minister's office. I could see the outer room was in darkness.

I rang Downing Street from the phone outside the Parliamentary Questions Office and my call was answered by a familiar voice that I had often spoken to before being put through to the Prime Minister's office. I asked to be put through to Peter Morrison, who was by now Margaret Thatcher's bag carrier. The switchboard operator said he'd gone home.

'Gone home?' I yelled. 'This is the most difficult day for the Prime Minister... and he's gone home?'

'Yes.'

'I think I'll come over and see the Prime Minister,' I said.

'I think that would be a good idea,' said the kind voice on the switchboard.

I gathered up some work and went straight over to Number 10 where TV cameras started running as I walked through the door. I asked for Peter and was again told he wasn't there.

'It really doesn't matter. I've come to see the Prime Minister,' I told the doorman.

He seemed rather startled, and a duty clerk was called down, who explained that Mrs Thatcher was preparing her big speech for tomorrow and probably could not see me.

'It doesn't matter; I'll just wait.'

'It will be hours,' she replied.

'I've brought work with me... I'll just be in the waiting room.'

I made my way in, but took the gilt off the gingerbread by thinking the waiting room was in the same place as on a previous visit. I went to the waiting room in which I had sat at the beginning of the summer before seeing the PM about Lairds. The fly that buzzed about then in a mad, undirected way had since died. It was quiet.

A messenger came and asked if I would like coffee. I asked for a black coffee, as I guessed I was in for a long wait. Then a political secretary came down and asked if I would like to write a note. I answered that I didn't want to write a note thank you, but wanted to talk to the PM about what was going on, and was happy to wait until she was free. Like a child, I showed him that I had work to occupy myself, and assured him I was happy to sit and wait and work.

'You are remarkable,' he said. And left.

Not long after, while I was on the phone on an outside line, Norman Tebbit came in to say that he could not make tomorrow's evening meal as planned. I walked up to him, in the bright overhead light, and said that I had come to see the PM because I wanted to advise her to resign, and that in sharing this information I guessed he would block my entrance to her.

'That's exactly what my message was,' he said. 'Frank, there was a time when I wanted to lead this party, and at one point I thought I could lead it. But now I see a party I don't want to lead.'

I said that the whole thing was out of control, a mad virus had gripped them and they were now a tribe.

He went off, and the Prime Minister entered, frailer than I had ever seen her. In an attempt to be business-like, she asked me why I was there. I gently held her in my arms and said I had come to talk about her. In the past she had been unbelievably kind to me, and it was now my turn to act kindly to her. She sat down on the other side of the table, and I put my chair at right angles to her. I said that it was so unfair, that she had never lost any election, and yet they wanted her to go.

My report was that Heseltine was over at the Commons like a Hoover, scooping up votes. There were people who had never dared say boo to her face, who were now moving off into the night to destroy her. I begged her not to go into the ballot, for she would be humiliated on Tuesday if she did. She said people were not giving her this information... it was being kept from her.

She added, however, that she had suspected what was happening. What was she to do? My suggestion was that she should go into the second ballot and then, at the end of the Commons debate, announce that she was withdrawing in favour of one of the two candidates who could succeed her. I stressed many times during our short discussion that she could not survive as leader, but she could determine the succession.

If she went into the ballot and prevented other candidates going in, when the tribe wanted a wider choice than her and Heseltine, they would undoubtedly elect Heseltine. She could stop that. She said she was anxious to prevent Heseltine because he was so unsuitable.

'Who do you suggest I should support then?'

'As leader?' I said, 'clearly, John Major.'

'He is so good... but young,' she mused.

'You can't always hold that against him.'

I didn't discuss the tactics of how she might do it: of her proposing him and Douglas Hurd seconding, nor of her announcing her successes on the international scene: the closure of the Cold War, and beating the vile, bullying trade union side in this country. And yet, with all these achievements, and three general election successes under her belt, she could not secure the one victory she needed, the overwhelming support of her colleagues, which would be a knockout for the opening of the debate. In all the events, I forgot to mention this – and of course time was pressing.

The door was ajar for the whole of our interview, which must have lasted for half an hour, and I think Tebbit was listening to the whole of our conversation. He came in, beaming, to take her back to her work. And as she thanked me, her eyes again filled with tears. We moved into the hall, with its silent, grey-suited men. Yes, the grey-suited men were there, but these were the messengers, waiting in the shadows to open and shut doors. Ironically, they did neither, and Mrs T opened and closed the doors behind her.

She arranged that I should be taken out into Whitehall and not go past the cameras in Downing Street itself. She, as always, was ever thoughtful of my political skin. But as we moved out of the Waiting Room where we had talked, I asked her to agree a statement for our big meeting at Lairds next week. For the first time, in all the significant meetings I have had with her – and forgivably so, because she was thinking about herself and not me – she said, 'Let me get through tomorrow first; I have to make a decision early in the day if I am not going to stand.' That was a point she had made repeatedly during our short interview.

Before disappearing back into her office to work, she thanked me again for coming and said what a Christian act it was. I replied that it was nothing of the kind. Again, her eyes brimmed with tears. I left her with one message.

I begged her not to live just for the next few days, but to remember the last eleven or so years, and all the successes. In the worry over the next twenty-four hours, not to bring the temple down with her, or all her successes.

I told her I had prepared her profile entry for *The Sunday Times 1000 Makers of the 20th Century*. The achievements I listed were ones that no one could take away from her, and they were important for her to remember during the next few hours. I haven't given enough weight in this recall to the couple of times I emphasised that she couldn't win on Tuesday, but she could stop Heseltine and determine the succession. Nor have I mentioned at all how I described my feelings during that last week, as I saw her being destroyed publicly. Although on some issues we disagreed politically, it had made me ill: I could not eat properly. I had been sick at watching the spectacle of people who owed their very presence in Parliament to her, behaving in the way they had behaved. Early on in the conversation, the Prime Minister said it had been quite a strain being over in Paris when getting the news. The other leaders, she told me, were sympathetic and understanding, but they could not properly comprehend what was going on. I said nothing had happened like this since Churchill was replaced by Attlee at Potsdam. She jumped in quickly to point out how that change had occurred as part of a general election. This was a parliamentary coup. I agreed, but reiterated that, however unfair, she could not now win that vote on Tuesday, but could decide the succession.

Lastly, I have forgotten to record the most obvious impression of the meeting.

While still dressed superbly, Mrs Thatcher looked frail, for the first time. Around the eyes and mouth there were the gentlest of quivers, the sort that I have seen when my grandmother and mother were nervous and drawing on a lot of courage. The tables had been totally turned. It was not I who was supplicant this time. Just as my mother, when trying to face up to something, listened carefully to what was being put to her, so too with Mrs Thatcher; or as I will always affectionately call her, Mrs T.

# Robert Maxwell

*'I'll destroy you. I'll destroy you. Do you hear?'*

What felt like a big fat finger was poking into my back just under my left shoulder. I was talking to Rupert Murdoch at one of his parties, for this was the time when Labour MPs believed that *News International*, if not the best thing since sliced bread, was at least a great power in the land that it would be foolish to ignore. That is still my view. I turned around to see who was doing the poking, and also who was doing the shouting.

It was Captain Bob, or that was how he styled himself on the baseball cap he was wearing. Turning back to Murdoch I asked, 'Who's your friend?' Murdoch laughed. Captain Bob stormed off, no doubt to start poking and threatening someone else.

I had met Maxwell in the glory of his *Mirror* empire's office in Fleet Street. This was when I was working at the CPAG and the *Mirror* was still a great campaigning newspaper; it took more than Maxwell to destroy such a glorious tradition. I was there to win *Mirror* support for CPAG's longer-term campaigns. He sat there surveying the whole world, which he clearly thought he owned. There was minimal movement of his arms. The rest of his huge body was motionless except for the mouth that was mounted in thick flesh, the type that comes from wealth and not from imposed poverty. He yelled as though we were deaf.

Peter Jay, his chief of staff,[1] was in attendance. Maxwell yelled, ordered and laughed about him as though he counted for nothing. 'How could Jay bear this?' I thought, as I surveyed this grotesque scene. Jay was a man of real distinction who had, as Economics Editor for *The Times*, changed the course of the debate in this country by his carefully crafted articles on monetarism. Long before Thatcher there was Jay. And Jay stood there, when he was not ordered to move, and took whatever the great bully threw at him. His face reflected the shame of a small boy, the shame of a small boy when his father bawls him out in public.

Maxwell was defeated in his Buckinghamshire constituency – subsequently represented by John Bercow – before I came into the House, and I did not give him another thought until he went missing big time. The press speculated that he had suffered a heart attack, or was drunk, when he fell from the back of his yacht and was doomed.

As Maxwell disappeared off his yacht in 1991, so too the pension funds vanished from the network of companies he owned, including the *Mirror*. Like all too many of these characters, Maxwell kept his companies largely offshore. Tens of thousands of pensioners faced ruin. I was Chair of the Social Security Select Committee and immediately announced an inquiry into the *Mirror* company

---

1. Peter Jay, economist, broadcaster and diplomat, was Maxwell's chief-of staff from 1986 to 1989.

pension scheme and its lost assets. Invitations were soon sent out to appear before the committee. That was the easy part. The wheels of justice, understandably, began to move more slowly.

Less slow off the mark were what were known as the 'Tory squires', that wonderful breed of MPs who have largely died out. They had come into the House of Commons simply to support the Conservative cause and Pitt had once described them as being crucial to the despatch of government business. They were not there to make trouble, or at least not in public.

On a few occasions, small parties of this group cornered me and began an exercise reminiscent of Bob Maxwell, with less poking, thank goodness, but with an equal anger in their red faces as they insisted, 'You must call off this inquiry immediately!' as if I could singlehandedly torpedo the flagship select committee system that had only just been established under Norman St John-Stevas's Commons reform programme. 'Have you got that into your thick head?' My actions, they insisted, could prevent a fair trial.

Shouting and threatening me, as the Trots were to find out, was not the best way to influence my actions. The Select Committee Inquiry would proceed. Peter Lilley, Social Security Secretary of State at the time, was also at work fast realising the limitations of putting all our recovery eggs, so to speak, in a single judicial basket.

Lilley was set on an innovative path to trace the missing shares that had been held in Maxwell pension schemes. He appointed John Cuckney who had been one of our great post-war spies, as later I learned from others. This businessman of note (because I assume he kept his contacts with the intelligence world) knew where many of the dead bodies were buried, so to speak, in companies who were trying to deny any legitimacy in the 'ownership' of the disappeared Maxwell pension fund shares.

A wonderfully courteous man, John's patience finally broke when, with a new-fangled technique he had been lumbered with, a judge was trying to persuade those companies to return their disputed ownership of Maxwell shares to their rightful owners. No shares were forthcoming. Exacerbated by this near year-long exercise, John sent for the main players. In what would have been his gently spoken and beautifully crafted sentences, John told the assembled pack of company bosses that they would not leave the room until the missing £220 million of shares was restored to the pension funds. The money was pledged that day.

On one occasion John talked about Maxwell's fate. He asked whether, from press reports I had read, I had registered that a second boat was in the area when Maxwell disappeared off his own yacht. I had heard it rumoured that Maxwell did not deny his closeness to the intelligence services, especially the Israeli Mossad. John implied that the other ship was Mossad's, and the theory was that Maxwell may have feigned a heart attack or drunken stupor, and fall off his yacht on the understanding that the Israeli secret service would whisk him away to a new life.

But Mossad knew, as did everyone who dealt with Maxwell, that Mossad might well be able to change Maxwell's shape and goodness knows what else, but one thing beyond the power of plastic surgeons was Maxwell's mouth. He could never be trusted to keep his trap shut.

So Maxwell was allowed to drown. Mossad picked him out of the water to check that he was dead and, in a momentary failure of performance, put him back into the water the wrong way up for someone who had drowned. The inquest came under much criticism over how it closed down, rather than opened up, questions. Maxwell was buried on the Mount of Olives in Jerusalem where exhumations are never allowed.

On a few occasions, I raised with John what I believed he told me. He was at pains to reassure me that I must have misheard him. Misheard *all* of that story? Where we both agreed was that, at last, Maxwell's mouth had caught up with him.

# Greville Janner

*'It's Grovel. Grovel Janner. Grovel by name. Grovel by nature.'*

I cannot now remember the first time John Vaizey[1] introduced me to Grovel Janner. Nor, sadly, did I ever ask him why he was so insistent on renaming him thus. The name seemed so appropriate once it had been uttered. Whenever I saw Greville, I lived in fear that I would blurt out the Vaizey version of truth.

Greville took on another, more sinister face, during the Maxwell Inquiry. It began when the House of Commons' Social Security Committee was interviewing the companies appointed as receivers to the Maxwell pension funds. Four companies were up for

---

1. Labour Party economist and academic, later Lord Vaizey of Greenwich.

questioning and each, to varying degrees, proved itself to be an expert rip-off merchant.

One of the smaller companies sailed under the rather grand title of Buchler Phillips. Each inquiry session began with my leaving the committee hearing to greet our interviewees. Here I would try to put them at ease, reminding them of the format of the proceedings – they had already been told in writing – and assuring them that they would do well.

I greeted Mr Phillips, did my little spiel and began to accompany him into the committee session when the top half of his body reared over toward me so that his mouth was near my right ear. 'I am a member of the party, you know,' he said in a loud whisper, fearing, I suppose that, should I be deaf, he needed to ensure what he regarded as vital information had registered with me while minimising the risk of others overhearing his comment.

I heard only too well, and anger welled up inside me. *You've had it, mate*, I thought. *The damned cheek of trying to persuade me that you should have different treatment as a Labour Party supporter.* We were not, as far as I knew, a masonic fraternity. And 'had it' he did, so to speak, as events turned out. But he would have got away more easily with his ill-gotten gains had it not been for Gerard Goodwyn who was pure gold. Gerard, or Ron, as he preferred to be called, worked for Buchler Phillips where he was undervalued in recognition of his extraordinary range of abilities, and certainly in respect to his pay.

As the inquiry got underway, I began to receive documents, all of which related to the suspect practices that Buchler Phillips were up to, but that also shone a light on the other receivers and their relationship to Buchler Phillips. Ron was providing the information, for example, that suggested Buchler Phillips charged the top staff rate for hourly sessions while largely using junior, and far less well-paid team members to do the actual recovery – although not much recovery was taking place.

Ron reported that this was common practice; all the firms were up to it. As the information from Ron flooded in, I sought a meeting with him – he had left a few coded messages to which I was able to respond. Here was someone younger than me, a much larger than life, swash-buckling cavalier if ever there was one. Here were aspects of character that I would have loved to have possessed. He was fearless and a considerable risk-taker, for he believed in his work and had mountains of talent in his mission to sort out injustice. Everything about him suggested an urgency and of living life quickly. From the range of information he presented to me, it was clear that he worked all too quickly and had a natural sense about locating the crooks of this world.

Post Maxwell, Ron moved to Finland, met his tall, beautiful blonde wife (no surprise there as this was the type of lady over whom Gerard lusted), began his family and, true to character, began exposing corruption.

Once into the home straight of our inquiry, I wrote to the key witnesses, this time Buchler Phillips, putting to them some of the information we had gleaned from our various sources so they had a chance to tell the committee their side of the truth. The noose was beginning to be drawn around Buchler Phillips's neck. Then Ron gave me copies of correspondence.

Ron provided me with correspondence between Buchler Phillips and, you've guessed, Grovel Janner or, using his full title: The Right Honourable Greville Janner QC MP. Under the St John-Stevas Select Committee reforms, a number of committee chairs went to Opposition members. Greville chaired the Employment Select Committee as I chaired one monitoring the Social Security Department.

Buchler Phillips had sent my correspondence to Greville asking him to draft replies so that he could best escape the allegations I was putting to him. As if that was not bad enough, Greville was charging

£5,000 for each reply, and here it was in black and white. One Chair was working to undermine the inquiry of another committee, both were Labour MPs, of sorts, and the service came at £5,000 a throw.

Here a weakness of mine comes into view. I didn't report Greville immediately to the Speaker. True, I was thrown by the treachery. But was that the reason I did not shop Greville? There was quite a gang in the Parliamentary Labour Party, or so I thought, who I felt hated me for not being what they thought a loyal Labour Party man. Their definition of loyalty was to put the best face on whatever daft deed the party was up to, whereas I always acted and focused on making the party more electable, no matter how unpopular it might be in the short run.

Here would be one Labour Party MP shopping another Labour MP, possibly getting him thrown out of the Commons, triggering a by-election that the party might lose. Was it this fear that prevented me cutting Grovel off at the knees? Or were there conflicting pressures on me? How anxious was I to protect my source from harm, whose identity would surely be exposed in the hullaballoo that follows any exposure? Or was I just anxious to keep the flow of information coming?

There is ever the danger of trying to put myself in the best light by writing about yesteryear. The truth is that I did not know then, and certainly don't know now, what combination of reasons were at work in me. All I do know for certain is that if I told another MP of these events, I knew that they would relay them pronto back to Greville.

Then, when there was a 10 p.m. vote one evening, I was in my office, greatly agitated though knowing not the cause. I couldn't work so I wondered if I should go home, which was only a short distance from the House? But it was raining. When the rain stopped, I went over to the House. It was now 9.15 p.m. and there was little point other than heading over to the Chamber for 10 p.m. I went home soon after the vote, only to see that the lights were already on. *Strange*, I thought, *when I left it was broad daylight.*

I unlocked the door and wham; the place was a tip. I called the police. A young team soon appeared.

'It's a professional job,' they exclaimed.

'Why?'

They had taken out a kitchen window, and yet the intruders seemingly wanted to convince us that this was another run of the mill job.

'Have you got a safe here?'

'No.'

'What valuables have you got?'

'None.'

'What else are you keeping here then?'

I went to the cupboards built under the huge bookcases.

I had not told the committee clerks about the Buchler Phillips–Grovel correspondence. I had put these papers on top of the file boxes. The thieves wanted to suggest that they had been disturbed by putting wine by the door to the terrace, which they had left open. But the door had rain on the inside. They had left before 9.15 p.m. and not at the point that I returned home.

When the Sergeant at Arms, our boss person, was told of the break-in (by the police I suppose), he asked to see me. Our Sergeant had been Ambassador to Jordan and was deeply knowledgeable of the ways of the Middle East.

'I would like you to meet officers of the Special Branch.'

'Why?'

'Robert Maxwell was not a very pleasant person, and he knew even less pleasant people.'

The Special Branch advised me about the particular dangers of continuing the Maxwell Inquiry. But I couldn't follow their advice. If I was not to be shot, which is what they informed me was one of the dangers, I should never put the light on without first drawing the living-room curtains. I never draw them in fact, and just hoped the shot would be instantly fatal. I couldn't live a life of always drawing the curtains before putting on the lights, and of seeking different ways of going to the House every day. Once I came out of the front door, there was the choice of turning right or turning left.

'Not much challenge there for a would-be assassin,' I told the kindly officer.

The action I did take, as soon as I heard that Greville was being made a peer after the Blair government had been formed in May 1997, was to write immediately to Jonathan Powell, Head of Blair's Number 10 staff, arguing that surely we would not make him a peer. I told Jonathan what Greville had done for money during the Maxwell Inquiry. Back came a reply. The blame was mine for not telling Number 10 sooner. 'But I've just learned,' I replied. 'If you hadn't been so secretive about who was to be rewarded by the new Blair government, I would have told you sooner.' Or, as I have only thought as I write this chapter, did Jonathan mean I should have spoken out at the time? No matter what he meant, the last laugh went to Greville when he duly received his summons to the Upper House.

# The Maxwell
# Brothers

*'How long will this suspension last?' demanded Mr Carman.*
*'We're obviously not going into purdah for the rest of*
*the afternoon, or if we were I would be surprised.'*
*'More economic than a court, so I hope,'*
*Mr Carman quickly replied with a big grin on his face.*
*'Well, Mr Carman, we are not paid by the hour here.'*

I was replying to George Carman QC (1929–2001) who was a renowned British barrister known for his exceptional courtroom advocacy skill. He had represented notable clients such as Ken Dodd and Jeremy Thorpe. At this point, in 1992, I was chairing the new Social Services Security Select Committee amid the Maxwell brothers' pension scandal, which involved the misuse of employee pension funds to finance failing businesses.

George was now appearing as Kevin Maxwell's counsel before the Select Committee Inquiry into the disappearance of the Mirror Group pension fund assets. The Grand Committee Room, then the largest committee room in the Palace of Westminster, had been decked out for a select committee hearing. While the TV cameras are now part of the makeup of committee rooms, the grand hall, as it then was, had been loaned two large cameras from under which came cables so thick that one could believe they were the support lines for deep sea divers.

The hearing was not without humour. I had gone over to the Grand Committee Room to check that, as far as humanly possible, sod's law would not apply today, of all days. As I came out of the committee room, there were Kevin and Ian, along with their two QCs, looking somewhat bemused by having to queue with all and sundry.

'Have you been offered a room to wait in?' I asked.

'No,' came Carman's reply.

I was angry. Even though I was sick at how the Maxwell pension victims had been defrauded I was also ashamed that, with all the staff at the Commons, the committee's witnesses were being treated in such a cavalier manner.

Before I could move, an attendant appeared as if from nowhere. He was one of an old school that has long since been replaced. Behaving as though he was an understudy for Uriah Heep, the attendant endlessly rubbed his hands together and asked if he could be of assistance.

'You can. Is there a waiting room for the Maxwell group, please?' I asked.

'No-o-o. There are noooo free rooms,' he replied.

'No free rooms in *this* place?' I countered. 'What's up here?' And I pointed to a small staircase. 'Isn't there a room up there?'

'There is, sir... but it's where the policemen leave their helmets.'

'Will the helmet room do?' I enquired of Mr Carman. It would. And up went the Maxwell party to wait among the orphaned policemen's helmets until the committee was ready to call them.

This little drama had usefully filled in the fifteen minutes or so before the committee was asked to attend for a pre-briefing. I sat with the clerk on the raised platform surveying row upon row of chairs awaiting their occupants.

The committee divided up the questions among themselves while I went up to the helmet room to bring in our witnesses. In strutted Mr Carmen with what he clearly regarded as his party. I began the hearing, as I always did, by asking the witnesses to identify themselves for the record.

Kevin and Ian identified themselves. Both of their QCs had given notice that they wished to address the committee on the role in English Law that a person charged could remain silent, and that silence was a legitimate form of defence. This was, of course, a narrower point than the rules governing select committee hearings. Here, before a select committee, it was less than clear whether witnesses who had not been charged, but who may be charged under civil and/or criminal law, had the right to remain silent. George Carman opened proceedings and argued, if the reader will forgive my paraphrasing, that the charges against Kevin were 'immediate', that we were on the 'threshold' of charges and that charges were likely 'to be laid soon'.

Mr Carman spoke for a good twenty minutes and was followed by Ian's QC, John Jarvis. Here the committee was treated, and it was a treat, to a different and much cleverer defence of Ian's right not to answer committee questions. But even Mr Jarvis did not press the weakness of the committee's position. One of our committee members had gone on the Radio 4 *Today* programme that morning and threatened the Maxwell Boys that, should they remain silent, the public would draw their own conclusions. Here was an opportunity for the committee proceedings to be brought down around our ears. That opportunity was, thankfully, not seized.

But in place of Mr Carman's bluster and sense of high theatre, Mr Jarvis was measured and low keyed, and in his reasonableness he lent over backwards to flatter the committee. Even more important was that, unlike Carman, he never gave the impression that Carman had given about Kevin, that Ian would face charges. Indeed, at one point he helped Carman out by giving a novel meaning to the latter's use of 'immediate'. 'Immediate', we were told, did not mean immediately, but was an event that might happen at some future stage – but equally might not happen – at the end of the Serious Fraud Office's inquiries.

By now all the Tory members of the committee had penned me notes that begged me to instruct an end to the session – even making points of order asking to be excused from proceedings. We were going nowhere fast, and were already in dangerous waters. For the first time I could see how Mr Carman, had he been cleverer, could play the committee. Up he could jump and say that simply by calling Kevin to give evidence of whatever he knew about the pension funds disappearance, poor old Kevin would no longer be able to gain a fair trial. I moved to prevent that opportunity as soon as these initial presentations were over.

I announced that I would suspend the hearing to consult with the committee membership on the two QCs' submissions. It was at this point that Mr Carman, whose eye was now firmly fixed to the television cameras, asked how long we would take in our deliberations. I replied to this question in the fashion that heads this chapter: we were not paid by the hour. The room filled with laughter and Carman joined in. He could be a graceful player when he wanted.

I then asked both QCs to take away four questions that I wished to pose, which had arisen from what they had said to the committee and about which they should intake instructions from their clients.

I added that the Maxwell team could return to the room where they had been stationed before the committee hearing. The Maxwell party and I laughed out loud at this thought, but no one else knew the story of the policemen's helmets.

The committee room was cleared, and our star witnesses went up to their helmet repository outside Westminster Hall. I told the committee that there was little point in proceeding, without mentioning my fear of how Mr Carman could try and spring Kevin to allow a 'no fair trial' accusation to be run. The committee immediately agreed. Back came our witnesses and the public, and I informed the assembly that the committee would not continue with its hearing at this stage.

Peter Roberts, then my agent in Birkenhead, told me the following weekend that he received a number of calls from Birkenhead's premier criminal classes following TV coverage of the hearing. They all wanted to know the name of Ian's brilliant QC.

Each of the callers condemned Carman. 'What a joker!' said one. 'We wouldn't even think of paying a QC to admit the case against us was so strong that we risked being arrested!' And they asked if Frank could tell them the name of that clever guy who knew how to represent Ian?

Kevin changed his QC for the trial; so did Ian. The Maxwells' firms were liquidated and after being put on trial, both brothers were eventually acquitted of fraud.

# Tony Blair

*'How can you live in this room? It's so dead and cold.'*
*'I don't intend to stay here long.'*

**M**y first one-to-one meeting with Blair was when he was safely ensconced in the Leader of the Opposition's room in the House of Commons. Since Michael Foot had led the Labour Party, the Leader of the Opposition had occupied one of the houses built into the redesigned Barry and Pugin House of Commons, before then moving into an inferior suite of offices in Norman Shaw North. Blair had asked me over to talk about a book I had written on welfare reform, *Making Welfare Work*. I was appalled by his office; it resembled a one-night stand hotel bedroom.

'How can you live in this room? It's so dead and cold?' I asked him.

'I don't intend to stay here long,' was his wonderfully revealing reply. The talk was of generalities. It always was.

'I agree with so much of what you write about taking welfare back to one that is earned.'

This was typical of his comments to me. Whether he had ever read anything I'd written was a moot point. 'I agree with so much of your work' was a wonderful cover. If pushed on specific policy that the work contained, he could always disagree if necessary, without giving away that he had not read much, or anything, of the text.

There was never any doubt in my mind that Tony Blair did agree with much of what I wrote and said on welfare reform. His was an approach I judged to be like mine, of primarily judging policy by his gut feeling. We both fitted easily into the English Idealist set of beliefs for personal conduct as well as the conduct of politics. Deep down, I believe he supported the sentiments that underlay my work.

As I left his office, Alastair Campbell (Blair's campaign director in the Opposition) was loitering in the corridor as if he meant to follow up my meeting. I learned later just how important Alastair was and how, no doubt, every part of the meeting had been choreographed together. Alastair was an old friend from his days on the *Daily Mirror*.

'He intends to make you Secretary of State,' was the brunt of Alastair's reinforcing message. Indeed, Blair had made that promise, and told me that he hoped to. It was never ever more than that.

'If he is serious, why doesn't he make me Shadow Secretary of State now?' I replied.

Blair had told me that I reached voters he couldn't. My appointment would be the clearest demonstration to the public that a Labour victory would be followed by serious welfare reform. I, like most people then, thought the election might be a difficult one to win, despite what the polls showed.

Alastair pondered and said, 'We should talk later.'

The later talk was one signalling retreat. The media would be signalled that I was on board by establishing a welfare reform group along with Gordon Brown, Ed Balls and Harriet Harman amongst others. The media certainly read the message they were meant to, although doubtless with Alastair's helpful direction. But, for me, this was a first taste that presentation could take precedence over a serious structured delivery of welfare reform by both shaping the machinery and selecting the personnel to deliver on that objective.

Blair had always been clear that he wished to make me Secretary of State in his first government, although there was never a cast-iron promise. That agreement, however, led to a phone call two days after the great electoral triumph in 1997, which was very much a Blair victory. It was his transformation of how so many voters saw the Labour Party that led to Labour's largest parliamentary majority. Despite his unpopularity after the Iraq war, I believe he could have won a fourth victory. I answered the phone. The voice from the switchboard was the same that had spoken to me the night before Mrs T resigned. This time the voice was to say that the Prime Minister wanted to talk to me. Immediately Blair was on the line.

Would I accept Minister for Welfare Reform? I was stunned. He continued that I had been made a Privy Councillor. It was wrong to say that I had asked for this privilege, as Peter Mandelson, Blair's liar-in-chief, has fed to the media. Poor as I am at being a party politician, I have never been in any doubt about Bagehot's division of the world into the dignified parts of politics, where power is paraded in fine clothes and cloaked by tradition, but has no effect or effective politics that help shape the outcome of governments. I enjoy the dignified parts of the constitution because they can teach politics to the wider electorate. One only has to look at the late Queen's role in this respect. Her merely appearing at an event conveyed a huge message to the media, who were probably totally innocent of her intent.

Blair went on to tempt me by asking if there was anyone I wished to work with as Secretary of State? Harriet Harman had been marked down for the portfolio. I could have Jack Cunningham if I wished. Was there anyone else I'd like to work with?

'I would choose Harriet if I was you', said Blair. 'She'll do as she's told.'

This she did precisely, but to Gordon Brown's orders, not Blair's. I told him I would think about the offer.

'How long do you want?'

'I don't know. I'll ring back when I have a decision.'

I literally didn't know what to do. I then thought the position of Secretary of State would be important to push through a welfare reform bill. I learned differently, of course, that these once powerful roles would be quickly gutted by a Blair government to dignified parts of the constitution (as Bagehot called them), where they were not to be endowed, as previous governments had endowed their secretaries of state, with leading great state departments with a central say in developing policy. Here was another aspect of Blair's failure to believe and act as a pluralist, or to understand that plural interests lead to policies with greater effect.

While Blair dubbed my work as 'thinking the unthinkable', I strove always and only to propose the workable, and it was the workable I longed to implement. I was pulled towards accepting, and yet I knew gut-wise it would be the wrong decision.

After pacing around my flat for what seemed like ages, I called Malcolm Wicks. Malcolm was the closest friend I had in Parliament before he died of cancer in September 2012. He was generous. He was hoping for the call I had just received. If I refused there was a chance that he would be offered the post, or at least a job in the government.

'You should take it,' he urged.

'I feel deeply unhappy... I don't believe that the arrangement will work,' I replied.

There was a call from Downing Street, the significance of which

I only understood some time later. At the other end of the line was Moira Wallace, who I knew was part of a very small permanent staff at Number 10. The Prime Minister wished me to come to Downing Street in the late afternoon.

'Where would you like your Rover to pick you up?'

I was puzzled. Rovers were the make of car allotted to Cabinet ministers. As my London flat was only a short walk away, I said I would make my way through the park to Number 10.

'Where would you like your Rover to take you after seeing the Prime Minister?'

I said I would walk back, I replied, asking why I was being asked about a Rover. 'And why am I being given a time to see the Prime Minister when I have yet to agree a position with him?'

'Whoops!' was the sound at the other end of the phone. 'You had better forget about this conversation.'

After a while the phone rang again. It was Jonathan Powell, Blair's Chief of Staff asking if I was going to take the job. I told him I hadn't made up my mind.

'There'll be a reshuffle in six months. You know what that means, don't you?'

Jonathan wanted me to draw the conclusion that what was being offered was at best temporary. With his help, I too drew that same conclusion; but that is not how events turned out.

I still couldn't make up my mind, and told him I would ring back.

'How much more time do you need?'

'As much as it takes,' was my reply.

Between these calls I had contacted close friends and asked their advice. Although they unanimously advised that I should accept the offer, I still resisted. My gut told me it somehow would not work, and yet I knew how a refusal would be used to dub me, yet again, as not being a team player. Those comments, that I was never a team player, were always anonymous, but they hurt. The fact there was no team to play for when the Trots were at Labour's throat was too painful for the appeasers to recall. Team playing was highly valued, even when the team was leading the party toward an electoral precipice. Yet I believed what I was being offered would never work in practice. In my conversation with Blair, I had said that he would never be more powerful than he was now, and that he should make a Cabinet in his own likeness.

I paced around my TV-free flat. The elite members of the government had been announced – the Foreign Secretary, Home Secretary, Chancellor of the Exchequer and the Education Secretary – but there were no further moves on other Cabinet appointments as the TV commentators had expected. If I'd had a television I might have guessed – although I still doubt that I would have done – that the remaining appointments were being held up pending my decision. The commentators couldn't understand why ministers' names were not being machine-gunned at them. Perhaps I had a stronger hand than I realised.

In Donald Macintyre's book on Peter Mandelson, *Mandelson: The Biography*, Donald recorded that Blair had given a list of his Cabinet appointees to Peter two days before the election. The only name he objected to was mine, which had been put down as Social Security Secretary. I did not know this until long afterwards, when Donald Macintyre's book was published in 1999, but all the time I was talking with Blair I had the feeling that others, possibly Peter Mandelson and Gordon Brown, were present.

After an intolerable time pacing up and down, I phoned to say yes. Despite such misgivings, I felt real joy when making my first and only call to Downing Street that day. Sounds of joy greeted my decision. Would I go some time to the department to get briefed. I would be called over to Downing Street in the following week for pictures to be taken and the image of the key role I was supposed to play in reforming welfare would be relayed during news time. Thirty years of work was about to be followed by membership of a government committed to welfare reform along the lines I believed right for the country and that offered long-term success in transforming Britain.

When I went into the department, much later that evening, I was on my way for supper with John (historian) and Patsy Grigg. I walked through the new annex that joined the row of Georgian terraced houses that had once been the base of a newly created Cabinet secretariat when Lloyd George took over to counter our faltering war effort. Up the stairs I bounded into the Secretary of State's office. Staff were still there although it was gone 7 p.m. Smiles and claps greeted my appearance. I picked up a superb briefing pack on the good aspects and the weaknesses and challenges in the social security strategy as it then stood. It was an extraordinarily prescient piece of work, though not one the government totally followed. For the first time I felt excitement as I made my way to the number 53 bus stop in Parliament Street, facing what was then the Treasury building. On joining the bus queue, a group of friendly West Indian mums congratulated me on joining the Cabinet. Although I explained I was not a Cabinet member, it was lost on them. My name had been announced long before most of the Cabinet. 'You are surely in this body,' they said.

Any further speculation ceased as an over-full number 12 Routemaster bus drew up parallel to us, not taking on passengers but waiting for the lights to change so it could move left toward Westminster Bridge. Those buses had small four-inch windows and on that warm evening they were fully open. Through such a small gap, what looked like a twenty-year-old lad started shouting.

'You won't make us fucking work. You fucking bastard! You ain't gonna make us fucking work. You are a fucking bastard. Do you understand? How dare you call yourself a fucking Labour MP?' I thought this was a rather appropriate introduction to welfare dependency on my first day as Minister for Welfare Reform.

The diatribe went on and on. I longed for the lights to change so that my abuser didn't have a chance to get off the bus and bonk me squarely on the nose as I stood in the queue. At last, the lights changed and the bus began the rest of its journey toward Dulwich Library. One of the mums turned to me.

'I do hope you make people like that work. They live on the dole and we have to pay for it.'

The women were on their way home after a full Saturday's work and, I was sure, for hardly a handsome wage. A number 53 arrived that would take me to the Griggs' house in Blackheath and I, along with the rest of the queue of, dare I call them, genuinely hardworking mums, scrambled aboard. What a day that was.

# Geoffrey Robinson

*'Every Cabinet committee needed a Geoffrey.'*

We sat around the table, as did those bishops once upon a time attending their first ecclesiastical Commissioners' meeting.[1] Back then, the issue was redistributing ecclesiastical revenues away from the mega Prince Bishops and toward the poorest of curators. Our issue was welfare to work but we were as inactive as those bishops were, until our leader came. The committee was chaired by Gordon Brown as Chancellor of the Exchequer. The bishops had remarked

---

1. The first meeting of the Ecclesiastical Commission was held on 9 February 1835 under Tory Prime Minister Sir Robert Peel to consider the dioceses, cathedrals and parish incumbents, with a view to securing a more equal distribution of revenue and a more efficient Church.

that they sharpened their quilled pens while awaiting the arrival of Bloomfield, who was then Bishop of London. Then, as with a big bang, the work of the Commissioners began. So, too, with our welfare to work committee. In place of cutting quill pens, we tried to cover our aimlessness by talking of matters of the hour. It was only when our leader arrived that matters switched to the welfare reform agenda.

But our Bishop Bloomfield was not the Chancellor, who invariably sat in place brutally looking over the weak specimens before him. No, our leader was Paymaster General Geoffrey Robinson, and no business of any worth was initiated, let alone concluded, without his arrival and subsequent direction.

The media has dealt Geoffrey more than a chequered record. His leadership on the Cabinet committee was low key, reserved, but inspirational in outcome. What had once seemed impossible to our nominal chairman was more than crafted into a plan of operation. The object was clearly set out, and the route map to arrive at our destination was detailed. Those civil servants who wanted to do their own thing, or nothing in particular, were given their marching orders. And through the fog of inaction, a workable programme of reform began to take shape.

We were officially tasked with establishing pilot schemes that were designed to upskill young unemployed school leavers into tomorrow's workforce, and it was from these pilots that a national scheme would be rolled out. But I think Geoffrey was working to an unannounced timetable. I certainly was. By 1986, Labour had been out of office for thirteen wasted years.

Time was short. Many young unemployed souls needed rescuing. There wouldn't be time to evaluate our pilots before a parliamentary guillotine fell on our work. But, all the time, Geoffrey directed our attention to devising a pilot that could easily and workably become a national scheme. A national scheme began operation before the pilots were even complete, never mind evaluated.

To rephrase a well-known saying about Willie Whitelaw, every Cabinet committee needed a Geoffrey if it was to become an effective, as opposed to merely a dignified part of intra-party warfare. Quill sharpening ceased as Geoffrey set out the objectives for that day's meeting. Yet this side of Geoffrey is never mentioned, let alone stressed, when his much talked- and written-about business deals are so eagerly dissected.

# George Carey

*'I don't know what's going on, but if you wish to be Second Estates Commissioner, I, too, wish you to have this position.'*

In 1997 the government was already functioning in a normal fashion, at least to outside observers. During my fateful conversation, when Tony Blair was trying to persuade me to join his first government, I was asked if anything would persuade me to join his team – apart from being Secretary of State. I replied that if I joined as Minister for Welfare Reform, this post he said he had specially created for me, I would also like to be Second Estates Commissioner.

'What's that?' replied Blair.

'This office-holder speaks for the Church Commissioners in the

Commons (and, to people in politics, this person speaks for the Church). Might I undertake both tasks please?'

'Is it mine to give you?' came Blair's reply.

'It most certainly is.'

'Then you shall have it.'

The Archbishop of Canterbury, Robert Runcie, had by then co-opted me on to Synod, but my support for women priests, however, led the Catholic group on Synod to block any renewal of this offer. I was not, therefore, a member of Synod – but I was getting used to being deselected for posts.

The debacle over the Church Commissioners' investment strategy was exposed by John Plender in a brilliant piece of reporting for the *Financial Times* on 11 July 1992. I moved to bring the Church Commissioners' investment strategy before the Welfare Select Committee, which I chaired. The Commissioners were the guarantee of clergy pensions and it was on that basis that our inquiry was launched.

Many members of Synod were affronted, I was told, for they didn't hold the view that I did on Establishment. The Church of England, by Establishment, was still in some real senses accountable to Parliament. Moreover, the Church Commissioners were responsible for underwriting the payment of clergy pensions, and the conduct of the First Estates Commissioner in losing £600 million in capital would be fully investigated by Parliament. This was another big red flag to the already demented Synod buffs.

I always believed that Philip Mawer, Secretary General of the General Synod of the Church of England, had taken against me. Courtesy, I thought, required me to inform him of the PM's decision to give me the Second Estates Commissioner role. So much for courtesy. The snakes in the Garden of Eden were at work. Ugly manoeuvring began behind the scenes, which led to that conversation in 1992 with George Carey, the Archbishop of Canterbury.

George's obvious distress that there was such unpleasantness behind the scenes, which I had been totally unaware of before his call, was followed by a long hand-written letter. It could not have been more kind and gentle. He told me that if I wished to be Second Estates Commissioner the appointment would have his full backing. He was not part of the campaign to block me, but he was trying to get to the bottom of who was directing the blackballing. He looked forward to us working together and I reciprocated.

I may have played a very little part in George's appointment to Canterbury in 1991, not that he knew. During one of my evening meetings with Mrs T, I informed her that she would soon be choosing a new Archbishop of Canterbury to follow Robert Runcie.

'How did I know that?' she asked.

'Because the retirement measure cuts Robert off at 70.'

'I shall ask for three names,' Mrs T batted back.

'You can't ask for three,' I replied. 'The convention requires only two. A royal commission will have to be established to make the appointment. You choose the Chair and there lies your power over the two names that the Commission will present to you. You need a Chair who will get a name you want into the archbishopric.'

Mrs T hinted that she thought the then Archbishop of York, John Habgood, was highly intelligent but she couldn't accept what she regarded as his relativist views. She had read his essays and was gently adamant in holding her opinion. Now, I thought, was not the time to overthrow that particular belief about John Habgood. After emphasising that the Chairmanship was crucial to the outcome, the conversation gave way to another.

Sometime later, a lead letter from Lord Caldicot appeared in *The Times* on the theme of capitalism and morality. That's the Chairman of the Royal Commission, I thought, and so it proved. Caldicot was based in the West Country. He did not know, I believe, much about the leading candidates for Canterbury but would probably know his own local bishop, George Carey, who had been appointed recently from a Bristol-based college. And so it proved. George Carey was one of the Commissioners' two names and George's name was quickly confirmed by Mrs T. Immediately, the appointment was met by a ghastly barrage of middle-class snobbery, and that is describing it in the best terms possible. He was not of the right class, whatever that meant. He didn't have an Oxbridge degree. Eileen Carey, George's loving wife, was said to have turned up to an event with the wrong gloves, whatever they should be. This barrage of snobbery left me stunned.

George's story was such a wonderful one to tell. He was an East End boy who had worked his way up, taking a first-class degree by evening classes. And that first-class degree was awarded in an age when they were as scarce as snow successfully invading the domain of hell – and from going to night-school at that. He was so clearly and hugely gifted that I thought the Church of England was lucky to have him as archbishop. If ever there was somebody who was going to talk to the nation in the nation's language, it would be him.

A friendship was soon forged during the select committee's inquiry into the First Commissioner's reckless gambling of Church assets. Two figures had much impressed the committee members during our inquiry into the present vulnerability of clergy pensions. The inquiry was, of course, into the much wider issues of the Commissioner's investment strategy, the role of the Church Commissioners in distributing the success of this investment, and the link between the money resulting from the investment and the buttressing up of the National or Established Church.

One person to impress was Sir Michael Colman, who was appointed quickly as the First Estates Commissioner to clear up the mess. Yet his start before the committee couldn't have been worse. He had a team of staff behind him, but when he turned to ask for advice he did not know their names. Bernard Jenkin, a key member of the committee, caught my eye and my spirits sank. But soon his humbleness and high intelligence won over the Commission. Here, if ever, was a safe pair of hands with a brain to go with it that would push forward reforms.

The second person to impress was George Carey himself. He looked under huge pressure as he appeared and, unlike Michael Colman, his staff sat with him alongside the table where witnesses for the committee hearing sat. No one was going to turn around for advice here.

He stopped the politics that had been rumbling in Church circles. He maintained that the committee had a clear right of sovereignty, to make this inquiry. He welcomed what we were doing. He and the committee were at one. He knew, and emphasised, that while foolish people said that the Church would soon make up a capital loss, he knew that loss could never be made up as the Church's returns would be forever and a day founded on a smaller capital base.

Select committees, which some view as outdoor relief for MPs, are sometimes prone to overplay their importance. But in George's hand our report was used to help reform the powers of the Church Commissioners and then the body that George established and named as the Archbishops' Council. Our aim was to reinforce the power of the archbishop at the expense of a noisy and disparate Synod.

Here was some background to the long hand-written letter from George Carey on my appointment as Second Estates Commissioner. George had worked as best he could to allow me to take office. And so I did, for the briefest of moments. I had not politicked over the appointment – or if I had it was in the naivety of telling Philip Mawer of my appointment. I now felt secure, given my conversation with George on the phone and receipt of his hand-written letter of endorsement.

I completely underestimated the serpents in the bureaucracy. Some weeks into the life of the Blair government, I was meeting with civil servants on welfare reform. The phone rang. Would I please speak to the Prime Minister?

Tony Blair was put through. 'You know that Church Commissioner's job, Frank? Can I have it back? I realise I've given nothing to Stuart Bell.' Stuart represented a constituency close to Blair's and had clearly been kicking up a fuss that somebody of such super intelligence as himself should have been rewarded properly with a middle-ranking, if not a Cabinet, office.

The wind went out of me. I had failed to shore up that position by squaring it again with Number 10 after the archbishop's letter. But the model I had hit on was that, while it was not already obvious that I would be on a collision course with Gordon Brown, I would work within the team and accept the decisions of those senior to me, to prove I was a fully paid-up team member. Here was a point that Gordon never seemed to appreciate and over which, it turned out, Tony didn't care. I believed that Gordon's plans of ever borrowing would soon be exposed and then a serious programme of welfare reform would start. I was wrong on the big issue too.

I replied to Tony Blair, 'What the Lord giveth, the Lord taketh away'. No laughter from Mr Blair, only thanks for giving him the room to unruffle ruffled feathers. That Blair's response to me was given without any hint whatsoever that he had picked up the humour associated with my reply and its source, began for me what became a longer-term doubt about just what Tony Blair did believe and know about Christianity. The serpents operating in Church House politics had won. I lost. And the role I wished to play in hopefully adding to George's programme of reform, and seeing those reforms through Parliament, were smashed to bits.

I still failed to read the 'right' lessons for survival in the Blair government. One was not rated by loyalty but by one's ability to fight like a rat in a sack, tearing at one's colleagues.

# Gordon Brown

*'I thought you were my friend, my friend, my friend!'*

That is what was being shouted as I was firmly gripped by my lapels and shaken like a ragdoll.

'I thought you were my friend, my friend, my friend... but you disagreed with me. You disagreed with me.'

'But I am your friend Gordon – that is why I disagreed with you,' I replied as best I could, for speaking while being violently shaken was a unique experience for me.

'My friend? My friend? My friend?' he yelled, as he dropped me.

It was the run-up to the 1997 election. Tony Blair wanted me as part of his team, as he liked to put it.

'You reach parts of the electorate that even I can't reach.' That was one reason that he gave to me.

'Why not appoint me to the Shadow Cabinet?' I asked, if that was the reasoning. He devised instead to establish a working party on which I would be a member. The message was to be spun that I was on board.

I didn't read the significance of his failure to make the obvious movements and get a clear-cut decision over my role on welfare reform in a future Labour government. That significance would dawn later, when I witnessed their decision-making abilities in government.

The working party met only a couple of times. There sat Harriet Harman with her new notebook. Ed Balls glowered over the proceedings like a none too happy Cheshire cat. Gordon made some suggestions on welfare reform. I responded that I didn't buy this package, it was far too complicated and, anyway, I wasn't sure whether I agreed with the thrust in the strategy underpinning the proposal – yet more means testing. We needed to move in the opposite direction, away from reinforcing the 'poverty trap'.

The meeting ended, I left the Shadow Cabinet room and walked along the corridor. This comes out into a stairwell beginning a floor above the Speaker's Garden entrance and rises several storeys. Blair and his Opposition team occupied one of a number of houses that had been built for senior staff members in the then new Palace of Westminster. As I made my way to the stairwell, I heard a rushing noise from behind. Before I could say Jack Robinson, I was pushed round and that's when Gordon began his shaking exercise. The 'I thought you were my friend' saga began. I was stunned. This man is mad, I concluded, as he loosened his grip. Gordon stumbled back toward the Shadow Cabinet room. 'My friend... my friend?' he kept mumbling to himself. As Gordon continued his mumbling, I vowed that, if it was the last thing I did, I would try to prevent this man from being prime minister. Another failed objective.

Before this display of physical power occurred, I had worked to try and establish Gordon's right to the leadership. When he and Tony Blair first came into the House, I, with so many other MPs, was struck by Gordon's Olympian-like qualities. From the distance at which I comprehended him he appeared to be the rising hope of a Labour Party that had not wagered too well with its fate since 1979.

Of course, there had previously been dark hints of what lay ahead, but I was too naive to read the signs. On one occasion the phone rang and, without me having a chance to say who I was, Gordon was raving down his end of the instrument and shouting that I was part of a plot against him.

The cause of this first warning shot was a letter I had sent to the *Guardian*.

'What on earth are you talking about? I haven't been talking with anyone... let alone plotting.'

'The letter to the *Guardian*.' He kept asserting this was part of the plot.

'No one suggested, let alone drafted, what I wrote.'

The row went on.

'I can't keep telling you,' I finally replied. 'I'm off to a conference on establishing a statutory minimum wage'.

'I don't know about the conference.'

'You should,' I retorted. 'You were invited. Jacques Delors has sent a handwritten note apologising for his absence. David Hunt (then Employment Secretary) replied that he is coming. All you did, Gordon, was send a printed postcard claiming a reply letter would soon be winging its way to me. It was untrue. I've heard nothing from you since. So, I'm off to the conference and I'll talk to you when I get back.'

And talk I did – or at least I tried. A date was arranged by his office, but no Gordon appeared. No appearance at a second arranged meeting either. A third date was arranged and, as usual, I took work with me in case of any delay. After about half an hour Gordon rushed in and began mimicking a caged lion. Round and round his office he went, lamenting that he thought I was his friend.

'Gordon, come and sit down.' He finally did. Again, I affirmed my friendship but explained that, while I thought he should lead the party, he was distant from his parliamentary colleagues and this much weakened his position in any future leadership contest.

I suggested he gave over one hour each week, on a Thursday, before colleagues made off to their constituencies; or at least those who took their constituency work seriously.

'Invite in six backbenchers so you can get to know them, but more importantly, they can get to know you Gordon. Give them a drink.'

'No one will come.'

'Don't be so stupid. They will.'

'Will you come?'

'Yes, I will come.'

'To each one?'

'Yes, to each one.'

'Will you give me a list of each batch of six?'

'Yes, I will do that.'

'And will you come?'

'I promise you.'

The list was duly submitted but nothing happened. The list was resubmitted, but to no avail. The last one was again resubmitted, and so it went on. Then, one Thursday evening, I met Malcolm Wicks and Tony Wright.

'You'll never guess where we've been,' Malcolm chimed, as if walking on air. 'We've been having a drink with Gordon,' was pronounced in a way implying that I hadn't.

'Only two of you?' I asked.

'Yes.'

He had limited our meeting to two, and his office had omitted to invite me! At this point, I confess, I gave up bothering trying to get Gordon to meet small groups of his fellow MPs.

Not that much later, John Smith, Leader of the Opposition, died. A leadership race was on and Tony Blair romped home as that ordinary sort of guy most of us thought would appeal to the electorate.

Once the Labour government was formed in 1997, I had little direct dealing with Gordon although I was conscious of being, with others, on the receiving end of his command control operations from the Treasury. On one occasion I went over to the Treasury to remonstrate with him over some cock-up he was trying to blame on the welfare department. He was fond of inventing initiatives that resulted in administrative nightmares. He had announced a winter fuel bonus to be paid either to individuals or married couples. Pension records are based on individual records, not on a household basis, so there was no obvious means of locating which were the two-person and the one-person pensioner households. I went over to talk with Gordon and tell him that he had set us a hell of a task. Yet he was adamant that he had been misled; the civil servants had not told him of this little local difficulty.

Throughout our meeting he sat looking away from me. We were getting more and more excited, but with Gordon blaming the civil servants. I assured him that they had given him fair warning. We were getting nowhere, so I concluded by trying to get Gordon to see that if he shouted and continued to shout at civil servants who he considered to bring bad or unwanted views, they would naturally shut up. Shutting up in those circumstances, after trying to put forward a correct record, was obviously not the same matter as trying to mislead a minister.

Perhaps the most terrifying and maybe the most notable run-in Gordon and I had was our confrontation over abolition of the 10p tax rate. This turned out to be Gordon's final budget and he planned to knock David Cameron off balance. He succeeded to some extent too. In a detailed eighty-one-paragraph speech, Gordon threw in, at the seventy-ninth paragraph, that he was reducing the standard rate of tax from 30p to 28p, and simplifying the tax system by moving to only two rates of income tax and removing the 10p band.

The cost of the 2p reduction was a little in excess of £8 billion. The additional tax paid by abolishing the 10p rate came in at £7.3 billion. In other words, a cut in the standard rate of tax benefitting everybody was being largely paid for by the abolition of the 10p rate, which overwhelmingly benefited poorer workers. The group that lost out most were single and married women, usually toward the end of their working lives.

I tabled an amendment, but there was little enthusiasm on our side for a fight as the measure was not to come in until the following year and after another budget. The day duly arrived when I was to move that amendment. The order paper had a number of amendments to be called before mine. I checked with the Whips. There would be a vote, they assured me, before my amendment. I could go about my business, and I did.

The debate on the amendment before mine was taking its time. A cold shiver suddenly ran down my spine. They'll not call a vote, I thought. They'll collapse the business on the amendment, the Deputy Speaker (who chairs the detailed debate on the budget) will call me and, if I'm not in the Chamber, my amendment will fall!

I started running from the third floor in Portcullis House, stumbled down the stairs, across the atrium, jumped as best I could down the escalator and ran fast along the open corridor that links Portcullis to the House, before clambering up the stairs to the Chamber. Breathless, I pushed the door open just as the Deputy Speaker was calling my amendment. Good-naturedly, he let me, panting, get to the third row behind the Treasury Bench where I always sat, to stand and move my amendment.

The Whips had not only tried to ensure I'd be out of the Chamber, and therefore unable to move my amendment, but Brown's attack dogs had ensured that I had no support. I said the issue wouldn't go away and that I would be back next year. The 10p abolition was not authorised by the House – I did not push my amendment to a vote.

One year on, I was better prepared. Or, in truth, hundreds of thousands of lower-paid women had got to work on their MPs. One colleague reported that she had been spied on by a group of disgruntled constituents who chased her down the high street. On the week I was to move the amendment to overthrow a key part of the budget, she and many more signed my amendment.

This was not the only show in town, nor the most important. Gordon's attack dogs had got Tony Blair out. The handover, if that's the word, was in progress. At one of their last appearances in the Commons, Brown and Blair left together, with Brown shouting out at me, 'I WANT to see you!' Innocents in the press gallery, who saw him communicating, thought he was about to offer me a job in his government. If they could have seen the expression on his face, they would never have entertained that idea.

After a short while I followed the Blair–Brown party, went past the Speaker's Chair, over toward the little corridor that houses the Chancellor of the Exchequer's room and, a little further on, the offices of the Prime Minister.

There was no sign of Brown. I strayed into his room and there, at a round coffee table toward the window, was sitting Hazel Blears. Her back was so straight that on that day she would have run the Queen into second place. *Aha*, I thought, *Hazel's landed herself a job in the Brown government.*

As I came out, Brown and Ed Balls were huddled together down the corridor. They crouched their shoulders over, thinking I would not be able to hear what they were saying, but they weren't successful. They were debating how to react to my amendment, and more specifically, to the parliamentary question I had put down for answer that day about the losers from the 10p change.

So, I moved further down the corridor into the Prime Minister's Waiting Room. The TV cameras were rolling – and were they ever not rolling for Mr Blair? Key footage was being shot covering Blair's last days in power.

I moved back along the corridor and Gordon beckoned me into his room. There sat Hazel. He gestured me over to another door and we entered what I like to describe as a cupboard. It was rather grand – it ran the whole length of the Chancellor's office to a room at the end – but it was a cupboard nonetheless. Gordon began by saying he was about to move offices – perhaps I knew – and here were some of his possessions. They looked more like rubbish to me, but each to his kind. Then his mood changed. He moved toward me, shoving his head toward mine. With eyes pierced, out came the charge that I had always hated him. And every time one of these confrontations occurred, I was thrown by the latest emission of bile.

'What are you going to do with your amendment?' he asked.

'It's up to you, Gordon. What are you going to offer?'

'I'm going to offer nothing. Nothing.'

'Then I shall move my amendment.'

'You will bring down the government.'

'No, I won't. But I shall press the amendment unless you give adequate compensation to the low-paid workers you've snatched money from.'

And I pushed my way out of the cupboard.

The next move was, of course, from the government. Alistair Darling, new Chancellor of the Exchequer, had met backbench rebels – although I was not invited. The Treasury Select Committee produced a report on the losers. Still I heard nothing, although it was clear that the government was panicking.

Then, on the day I was to move the amendment, Alistair Darling phoned. He outlined a package that would cost £4.5 billion and asked would I accept it. It didn't directly compensate the 10p losers. *How*, I thought, *could a government spend so much, and still not deal with those it had harmed?* The 10p group have never been fully compensated.

I knew it was too big an offer to keep our side together. No government had offered such a concession before. But the Whips were telling backbenchers that the government would fall if the amendment was carried.

There was no chance of that. I learned later that Alistair Darling had prepared a statement in case he was defeated. On defeat, the government wouldn't have resigned; it was absurd to think they would. Instead, quite sensibly, Alistair planned to come forward the following day with an amendment from which they would seek a vote of confidence from the House.

There were other run-ins with Gordon but none as important nor unpleasant as this one. How could a Labour Chancellor, just to wrong-foot Cameron, who had to rise immediately after the budget statement to give the Opposition's judgement, be prepared to harm some of the poorest workers in our society, for a quick moment of triumph? I still don't understand it.

# Basil Hume

*The cardinal was standing at the entrance of the beautiful*
*Bentley-designed church, behind Peter Jones.*
*'Frank, what a surprise to see you here.'*
*'I wouldn't miss Richard's re-ordination for anything,' I replied.*
*The cardinal laughed.*

As an Anglican I am used to the clergy meeting us after a service, not before. Here was the great Cardinal Archbishop of Westminster, Cardinal Hume, greeting the congregation for what was billed on the invitation cards as Richard's ordination, in 1995.

I had met Richard when I was attending the Edington Music Festival. The festival consists of a week of the most wonderfully performed church music at Edington Priory Church in Westbury.

Richard Marriott and Geoffrey Holley were staying at the St Denis's Community House in Warminster where I had lodged myself for a few weeks. Geoffrey made friends immediately and after breakfast we would be on our way to Edington. Geoffrey had a car and I didn't. Richard Marriott was an outstanding Anglican priest. His bishop, at the time John Waine of Chelmsford, said that he was the finest priest he had. But Richard was gutted by the way the Church of England was planning to make women priests, out of step with what he regarded as the more senior Roman Catholic Church.

The poor old Church Commissioners were called upon by the Church of England Parliament – the Synod – to make up to £50,000 compensation payments to priests who couldn't or wouldn't accept this reform. I was unsympathetic with these payments as I don't believe people should be paid to exercise their conscience. I did believe, however, that every adjustment should be made to accommodate a group of people who were witnessing the rules of the game changed in a way with which they might violently disagree and which they had never envisaged when they became ordained.

Payment as a form of compensation tests the conscience of the most robust. Perhaps, unsurprisingly, a small minority went about shaping their consciences to fit in with maximum compensation payments. Hanging around, to qualify under the number of appropriate years, would entitle a priest to stuff a £50,000 payment into their back pocket.

Richard was not part of this group. He had left on principle before any payments could be made. And, perhaps not unnaturally, events had swept Richard into the Roman Catholic Church. He had undertaken their training and, as the invitation card said, he was being ordained. I did not think for one moment that Richard needed 'ordaining'. He had been and was an outstanding Anglican priest, which he could never have been without already being ordained.

The ordination service started and before long there was a pause for the homilies. The cardinal said he had a duty to read a letter from Pope John Paul. It was appalling, denying everything about Richard's ministry, its validity, his importance, his local leadership; the love he had given to his congregation and that he had received back in such abundance.

Once this terrible missive had been read, the cardinal archbishop asserted that one of his privileges as a bishop was to preach his own text. Hume had a confidence and courage like no other public figure. The homily was short and wonderfully ecumenically centred. He said he wished to assure those who had received sacraments from Richard's hands yesterday that those sacraments were as valid as the sacraments that Richard would give tomorrow. Wham.

I long wondered afterwards whether I had heard correctly but I had to wait years for an independent source to verify what I had witnessed at that re-ordination. I was in Liverpool Heart Hospital, after having a heart attack on Friday, 13 March 2015. Patrick White, a Birkenhead lad and a Cambridge graduate, had looked after me beautifully for eight years as head of my office in Westminster, steering me free of trouble and organising the office in such a way that nobody realised they were being managed.

Patrick's father, Philip, from whom he clearly gained so many of his talents, showed me huge courtesy and beauty in visiting me, bringing me newspapers, the radio, and what I needed while I was trapped in hospital for the weekend after my heart attack. Patrick's father had been ordained a deacon but could not progress further to the priesthood as he was married. The unfairness that married Anglican clergy could come over into the Catholic Church and be *re-ordained* and practise as priests, while remaining married, I regarded as sheer nonsense although hurtful to people like Patrick's father.

During a lift that Philip had given me some time previously, I told him about the extraordinary homily that the cardinal had given during my friend's re-ordination service. Philip listened quietly and made no comment. I often wondered whether he believed that this was a sheer 'Fieldism', with my imagination in overdrive.

Over that brief weekend in hospital, Philip told me that he had met the Catholic chaplain, Father Jonathan Brown, as he was leaving the chapel to visit me. The chaplain told Philip that he knew me, and expressed his wish to come along a little later.

Philip went on to tell me that the chaplain was a former Anglican married priest who had become a Roman Catholic. During our conversation the now Catholic chaplain arrived. He challenged me by saying that I probably didn't remember him. He was right. He was gracious, however, in immediately saying that we met at Richard Marriott's ordination. 'Re-ordination', I corrected. He laughed and so did Philip. I took courage in both hands and asked the chaplain if he thought there was something special about Richard's re-ordination. He said there was. I asked him what was special. He said that after reading Pope John Paul's message the cardinal had given a homily in which he specifically told the very large Anglican congregation present that the sacraments given at Richard's hands yesterday were as valid as the ones he would give tomorrow and for the rest of his priestly life. It was worth getting over a heart attack to hear that 'story' affirmed.

# The Miliband Brothers

*David Miliband looked down on me in a superior way.*
*'I have yet to canvas you for your vote in the leadership elections.'*
*'Don't worry about that. I've nominated your brother*
*and shall be voting for him.'*

I met David Miliband on a few occasions, and particularly during the period when he was secretary to the Social Justice Committee tasked by John Smith, Leader of the Opposition, with formulating a new social justice strategy for Labour and one that went with the grain of the electorate. It was significant that Smith wanted a new approach; not for him a creation of New Labour. After John Smith's death, Tony Blair's ascendency in the Labour Party, his winning of the election and his installation in Downing Street in 1997, David was brought in on the incoming tide to the key job of running the Prime Minister's Number 10 policy unit. It was in this role that he called a group of ministers into Downing Street to discuss issues on which he said he sought advice. Such was the momentousness of the topics he wished to discuss that I have no recollection at all of what they were. David introduced the subjects for that day's agenda and went round the small group of ministers asking what they thought. The response was largely unanimous in supporting David's line, though a few of our band did question the position David wished to reach.

When David asked for my reaction, and I began to give it, his eyeballs rose into the top of his head and began rolling around. My response to this was that if David wished to tell me what he wished to hear, I would happily recite the appropriate ditty back to him; I added that it had taken Mrs Thatcher eight years before she reached the conclusion that it was distinctly unimportant to listen to views that were critical of hers. I congratulated David on reaching this position in a mere eight months.

Hence my response in the House of Commons coffee bar when David nonchalantly approached me about bagsying my vote. There was no way I was going to vote for somebody who showed a strengthening of his arrogance rather than any development of the humility that a leader of the Labour Party needed if they were going to successfully bring together those different factions that were fast emerging in the party.

The 2010 leadership contest between the Miliband brothers, as it turned out, couldn't have been closer. Sadiq Khan, now Mayor of London, managed Ed's campaign. He cleverly concentrated much of his effort on gaining MPs' second preference votes if they were not inclined to give Ed their full support. It was on the basis of second preference votes that Ed was carried to victory on the narrowest of margins on 25 September.

How would Ed respond to the challenge that political parties cannot survive if they simply deny all the benefits they have delivered during government, at the same time needing to learn from their defeat if they are to be successful in ever regaining power?

A crucial balance must be struck between bush-firing your own government's record, and thereby destabilising voters' perceptions of your party's achievements and competence, and adopting a policy that tells voters that the party is not listening to what voters are trying to say through the ballot box.

Over a long period of time, Labour's traditional voting base had been haemorrhaging. Their once bedrock of support among the white working class was being masked; at first, by voters simply abstaining. And then the red wall came crashing down. Labour's ruling elite went around whistling as though they were some of the rougher characters from a *Just William* story and chuntering that the disaffected sods had nowhere else to go.

Labour's open-borders immigration policy put a halt to a large part of dissatisfied Labour supporters' willingness to do anything that harmed the party – even though they would give up actively supporting it at the ballot box. We were lucky with the extent of the residual loyalty. In some areas our voters claimed they were being swamped by new arrivals, as indeed they were. In return, we lectured them not to use such language despite the truth that, over a short space of time, immigrants were indeed challenging and outnumbering the host community. Waiting lists for housing went up, NHS queues lengthened, families could no longer be allocated the school of their choice for their children, and wages were held if not depressed.

To the growing crisis in living standards for both white and black Britons, Ed and the Labour Party remained oblivious. I believe this remains true of the Labour movement today.

I made a mistake in believing that Ed Miliband's leadership would be open and that he would be anxious to learn rather than to assert. How wrong could I be?

All too soon we learned that Ed does do the listening bit, but he also loved conducting seminars at which every view was left in the air until the next seminar was arranged. Missing was any willingness to act on those areas of policy that revolted so many of our voters.

A key issue Ed had to decide as Leader of the Opposition was the party's response to the previous Labour government's policy of granting new European accession countries an unrestricted/free access to Britain's labour market, unlike our existing partners. They very quickly exercised their right to place temporary restrictions in the way of mass migration. We were the one labour market that was left open; and so the great rush began.

I couldn't decide the reason for Ed's line. Was it because he thought that no new script was warranted? Or did he see the immigration issue as a right-wing plot got up by the *Daily Mail* and the *Sun* that had to be resisted? Of course, immigration is an issue that right-wingers raise, but they capitalised on the issue to an unacceptable degree as the centre-left persistently continued its denial of what was obvious to any MP who paid the slightest attention to what voters were saying in their constituencies. Labour's vote continued to haemorrhage to UKIP. Ed continued to stubbornly maintain that his critics were misreading the scene.

I raised immigration privately in his office on a number of occasions. Cautious as ever, Ed treated these occasions as a seminar. I would talk. I would leave. Nothing would happen. So, I ceased to accept the invitations to these one-to-one meetings with the leadership as I was wasting Ed's time. Ed raised my response not to accept further invitations, and it made little difference even when I told him that there was no point coming because he was in tutorial mode, and not the mode of a leader presiding over a party whose vote was haemorrhaging.

He pleaded for one more chance for me to persuade him otherwise, or vice versa, I suppose. I turned up at the appointed time only to be greeted by his staff and informed that he was undertaking the most fundamental Shadow Cabinet reconstructions. Might I come back later? I agreed. I came back later. The restructuring was still in progress. Might I come back later? I came back later. The fundamental restructuring was still being undertaken. Might I come back later? I agreed that I would come back at half past six that evening. We had a seven o'clock vote and this would, hopefully, give us half an hour for discussion.

Coming back at half past six I found that the Shadow Cabinet re-structuring was still underway. I asked what the restructuring involved, thinking it must be something earth shattering. I was told that Lucy Powell was going to be given responsibilities as deputy to Douglas Alexander in a general election campaign and that my then neighbour, Alison McGovern, would be the junior shadow spokesperson for children. Wow. All day spent on that restructuring and yet it had still not been publicly announced. Would the voters be bowled over by these announcements? Could this be a foretaste of how Ed would have acted decisively if he ever became prime minister?

The office pleaded with me to give another date, preferably on a Friday. I explained that practically every Friday I was in Birkenhead but occasionally that wasn't the case. We fixed a Friday morning appointment.

The time came and I duly appeared in the office. There was no Ed Miliband. He was having his hair cut. Would I mind waiting? I brought work with me and I went into Ed's office and sat on one of the sofas and began working.

Sometime later Ed appeared and sat down beside me. 'Are you loyal to me?' was the first question he fired at me. I replied that I was *now*. 'What do you mean "now"?' shouted Ed. I replied that I had been trying to persuade Alan Johnson to stand against him so that we could have a chance of winning the election. But I had failed. So I was loyal NOW. Up jumped Ed pulling at his rather fine head of hair and shouting all sorts of messages about disloyalty. I tried to calm him down and make the point on immigration.

The response was that Ed would raise the issue at a Monday evening meeting of the whole Parliamentary Labour Party. Here was my opportunity to put up or shut up. The appointed day came. Ten of us had been chosen to speak. Eight of the ten back bench members responded, cheering and expressing their confidence in Ed, wishing the public could see more of this side of his character and hear the speech we had just heard. A number added that they hoped he would visit their seats during the general election campaign. It was a feast of brown noses if ever there was one.

Two of us disagreed with Ed's stance. Helen Jones, fellow Merseyside MP, made the case that we have rightly heard much of since. Very calmly, but wonderfully powerfully, she pointed out to Ed that the North London elite flavour of his shadow cabinet did not run well in her constituency, nor anywhere else where we had to regain our haemorrhaging working-class vote. An unrepresentative party had been created, which was increasingly ignoring working-class people's interests.

I came to speak, and I asked Ed whether he believed that opening the borders, and allowing five million newcomers into the country, had or had not had an effect of pushing wages down, of lengthening housing queues, of extending waits for NHS treatment and making it increasingly impossible to get the school of a family's choice in certain areas.

As I was posing these questions, a few MPs began growling at me. I didn't have the courage to tell them what I really thought: that huge swathes of them would not be back after the next election. UKIP would take votes from them and their seat would fall to the Tories or to UKIP itself. I did say that I knew not all of them would be back to greet me in the new Parliament if they intended to clearly represent these views on immigration to their voters. Following Brexit, the Tories capitalised on this discontent and almost wiped Labour off the map up north.

Ed replied to each of my questions. He said he could see no connection whatsoever between Labour's open doors immigration policy and falling wages, lengthening NHS queues, the impossibility of gaining a home for an increasing number of families, or the closure of the best local primary school to residents who were born and bred in the area.

Cheers resulted from Ed's extraordinary rebuff. The meeting was declared closed and individual members filed out quickly. I slumped into my seat. *How can I possibly be a member of a party whose views are so at variance to the interest of its core voters?* The thought kept smashing inside my head. I was so distressed that I had failed to notice a group of Labour peers who had come over to me. Joyce Gould, who had done so much to defend the party from the Militants, was one of the group; so was Bill Jordan, one-time leader of the then Electrical Trade Union. This small group assured me that although they had never stood in parliamentary elections, they understood precisely what I was trying to say about the growth of Labour's disaffected working-class vote.

Ed Miliband, stubbornly, did not change his stance. We went into the 2015 election only to find that nearly a million voters who previously supported us had easily converted over to UKIP. Ed was soundly defeated in the election, returning one of the worst-ever election results. He immediately resigned, but not before changing the membership base of the Labour Party so that people willing to pay three pounds could join. By doing so he opened up Labour to an unimaginable danger.

# Philip Green

*A friend told the* Daily Mail *last month, 'Frank Field is behaving like a complete arsehole, and Philip has no intention of appearing before his stupid committee. He hasn't committed a crime, isn't running away from anything and he's perfectly willing to help find a solution to the BHS pension fund's problems. So, it's laughable to say he ought to be stuck in front of some sort of inquiry. He's not about to be strong-armed by a load of tosser MPs.'*

Sir Philip Green, of course, turned up before the joint meeting of the Work and Pensions and Business, Innovation and Skills Select Committees. For days the media buzzed about the clash. I was scared, not by any physical threat; rather, my worry was that Sir Philip might run rings around the committee. Others were too, and briefing sessions were hurriedly arranged to hone the committee's skills.

The day of our meeting with Sir Philip arrived and we followed normal procedure for the Work and Pensions Select Committee. We met in private with our colleagues and shared out the topics and questions. I then went off to meet our witness, to explain how we operate, and to bring him into the committee room.

Witnesses are normally lodged just outside the committee room. Not so this time. Here was another similarity with the Maxwell Boys, who naturally wanted a room to wait in and were given one that housed police helmets.

'Where is Sir Philip Green?' I asked. The police said he was lodged in an interviewing room with his lawyers and advisers. At the door was an individual with shoulders so huge that he probably had to enter a room sideways. Inside were two similar looking gentlemen who turned out to be Sir Philip's ex-SAS bodyguards. *Does he really need special protection to walk the streets of England?* I wondered. Or were they a fashion accessory, like a very, very expensive handbag that tells everybody of one's arrival among the super-rich? The room was stocked with advisers, lawyers and general hangers-on.

I was shocked at how small Sir Philip was. In my mind's eye I had a picture of him that, from the start, was slowly being burnt like an old photograph. When the British Home Stores crisis erupted, I believed Sir Philip Green should be protected, seeing him as a working-class lad doing well in snobbish England. I believed he would have a good story to tell and that he would have little to answer for. How wrong was I? I became part of the re-education on Sir Philip Green that was happening nationally. Indeed, when I proposed to the select committee that we should undertake an inquiry into the BHS collapse and its impact on pensions, I did so because I thought we might have a good story about him to tell, or that he would soon make it a good story.

At that time, in 2016, the Work and Pensions Select Committee had a Tory majority – to mirror that in the House of Commons. Afterwards, members of the House told me that they thought this was an example of one of the bees in my bonnet. But they agreed to the inquiry because all members choose topics for the committee, and they kindly didn't exempt the chairman.

Hours after the announcement of our inquiry, I took the first of a small number of anonymous phone calls, which continued for about ten days. All of them were useful, particularly those that told me to look at the British Home Stores' supply chains that were supposedly rigged to enhance the stores' profits in the early years, and would shed light on how the rigging had been done.

I had struck a deal with Sir Philip not to call Lady Green before the joint committee and had done so for two reasons. First, our sister committee was locked in a battle with Mike Ashley of Sports Direct, who was refusing to appear before them. To have two chief witnesses putting two fingers up to Parliament could have been the basis for a major and unnecessary confrontation. If Sir Philip appeared, I reckoned that Mike Ashley would act similarly.

My second reason was better judged. I believe Sir Philip loved walking away believing he had struck a bargain. He would come if his wife was spared appearing. He came and she was given an immunity, if that's possible, by the Work and Pensions Select Committee. But our committee had no say over our sister committee for Business, Innovation and Skills. They were not party in any way to this agreement and could still be free to call Lady Green if they so desired. This was a point that Sir Philip had missed. But he had his bargain long before I realised that the principal driver of the whole of the Green family business was Sir Philip himself. So, we had the mover and shaker of the Green empire. If anything, I underestimated the control he exercised over this empire, making poor old Napoleon look like an emerging democrat.

I explained to Sir Philip the rules under which the committee worked, as I do with all witnesses. Part of me longed for our chief witness to open the proceedings with a statement that he had fully 'sorted' the pension deficit in the day or two prior to our session and that he wanted to have a serious discussion with the committee on the problems that beset all too many occupational pension schemes. For these problems are only too real.

The session lasted six hours. Sir Philip's line was not as I anticipated, which had been to lay out a plan of action for dealing with his pension crisis and thereby set the scene for national pension reform. It was, rather, to show his true character of abuse, evasion and attempts to control, by abusing committee members: 'Stop looking at me!' or 'You look far better with your glasses on.'

The three members of the Work and Pensions Select Committee were superb, far outclassing any questioning I could have made. None of their questions would have been relevant had Sir Philip followed the course I thought he would take, but so began a series of questions that led to the undermining of Sir Philip Green's empire, his confidence, and his position in public life. Let me stress again that none of this would have emerged had he followed the course that a normal human being would have followed in the hole Green had dug for himself. Now we were about to find out about that digging programme.

Jeremy Quin was alpha when it came to quietly ripping apart Sir Philip Green's story over the accounts, the movement of properties and loans. Karen Buck disarmed him with a combination of charm and iron. He clearly wasn't used to being answered back, least of all by a woman. Richard Graham, who has a vast knowledge of the financial world, was as charming as he was deadly with his questioning. The whole committee remained unruffled despite Sir Philip's rudeness.

While the report was being prepared, the first of three Sir Philip-inspired go-betweens contacted me – at least I imagine they were initiated by Sir Philip. I reiterated to them my disappointment that Sir Philip hadn't seized the initiative, walked out of the room smelling of roses and set the whole of British industry on fire with his contribution on the future of occupational pensions – the financing of which he understood only too well. Each of the go-betweens had a real wish to prevent Sir Philip further damaging himself and his family.

That came through clearly in conversations with the business journalist Jeff Randall, in which I was told Sir Philip would not go beyond £220 million, even though he had ended the committee hearing by promising to 'sort the pension fund'. Sir Philip, during the committee hearing, and through his go-betweens, stressed a wish to sort the issue, but in a manner whereby all his money only went to the pensioners, which I thought at the time was rather absurd. On each occasion I explained that Sir Philip couldn't make a settlement with me alone, but only with the Pensions Regulator, although I could give some guidance about the sort of sums that might satisfy the select committee members.

The agreement Sir Philip made with the Pensions Regulator to the BHS pensions fund of £363 million was lamentable. The charge sheet against him was so strong that he should have paid up every penny to ensure that no pensioner was ever made worse off by his plundering of BHS. So that fight is continuing, as is the fight with his fall guy, Dominic Chappell.

# Elizabeth, Baroness Butler-Sloss
## IMPRESSIONS OF FRANK FIELD

I first met Frank in 2000, when I had just become Chairman of St Paul's Cathedral's new Advisory Council. Frank, who was then Chairman of the Cathedral Fabric Commission and very knowledgeable on the whole subject, became a most valuable member of the Council. From there we became friends; my husband, Joe, and I dined with him; and he with us. In 2006, having retired as a judge, I was appointed a crossbench member of the House of Lords.

Anthony Steen MP and I set up the All Party Parliamentary Group on Modern Slavery and later the Human Trafficking Foundation, and Frank became a member of both. He did not join several MPs and peers who visited European countries to attend modern slavery conferences but he kept in touch with all our conversation and actions.

Impressed by this, in 2014, Frank approached Theresa May, then Home Secretary, seeking to persuade her to introduce a Modern Slavery Bill to Parliament. She told him to persuade her why she should do so and Frank's response was to recruit me and John Randall MP (now Lord Randall of Uxbridge) to work with him to produce a speedy report to convince Theresa that there should be such a bill.

Frank proved a taskmaster. We worked, often throughout each day, in October and November 2014, receiving volumes of information and hearing a great deal of oral evidence. In six weeks we had produced a report, which was presented to Theresa at the end of November.

She was persuaded by it, and the Home Office draft was ready in January 2015 and sent to a Pre-legislative Scrutiny Select Committee of both Houses of which Frank was Chairman and I was his deputy. We wrote another report for the Home Office in March 2015, and rather cheekily drafted our own version of the Bill, which, of course, was not accepted by the Home Office although some of our suggestions were included. The bill got support from across both Houses and became law in May 2015, after which the Home Office produced excellent statutory guidance. In its day, this was the first legislation of its kind and was not only applauded across the world but also copied by several countries.

Meanwhile, I became chairman of the Ecclesiastical Committee,[1] a statutory committee of both Houses, of which Frank became a most useful member.

In 2019 Frank recruited Maria Miller MP and me to review the working of the Modern Slavery Act of 2015 and how far it had been implemented. We composed a report to the Home Office containing a considerable number of recommendations, many of them the government accepted. However, those that were accepted have not yet been implemented. On the contrary, since 2019 there have been three Acts of Parliament that have largely eroded the 2015 Act. Frank was acutely aware of all this and, despite his increasing ill health, he was in frequent discussions with several of us to look at what, if anything, could be done.

I visited him from time to time at his flat and discussed many issues with him. He was always on the ball and very aware of what was going on. He was an exceptionally kind and thoughtful friend. One

---

1. The Ecclesiastical Committee examines draft measures presented by the Legislative Committee of the General Synod of the Church of England. It comprises fifteen members from the Commons and fifteen from the Lords.

example was his friendship with Margaret Thatcher, in some ways a surprising friendship, but not surprising for Frank. He told me that he used to go to tea with her after she retired, but also mentioned that her former colleagues seldom visited.

After losing his Birkenhead seat in 2019 he was created a peer in 2020, and sat as a crossbencher. He managed, despite poor health, to attend the House occasionally.

I last saw him a few weeks before his death. Daniel Sanchez, who was such an enormous help to him as his aide-de-camp over several years, was with him. I took along several parliamentary documents and we discussed the next time he would come to the House. We were trying to put down an Oral Question on modern slavery to give him an opportunity to ask a supplementary question, but, sadly, he was not well enough for that to happen. It would have been a very uncomfortable question for the minister, whatever it was.

There are very few people with whom I have worked, and almost none in Parliament, for whom I felt so much respect, admiration and affection. He is so much missed by so many, and certainly by me.

# Kate, Baroness Hoey
## IMPRESSIONS OF FRANK FIELD

Although Frank had left teaching at Southwark College in Waterloo, London when I started my first job there in 1972, his name came up constantly in staffroom chats. The principal, Norman Dark, was a wonderful man, with a leadership style that involved taking a genuine interest in all his staff and not just their lecturing abilities. He soon became aware of my interest in politics and mentioned that Mr Field still popped into the college now and then, especially if he was in the area and needed to use a phone.

Sure enough, I saw him in the staffroom one day and struck up a conversation. It was the beginning of a friendship that became ever stronger as time passed. I fought my first general election in 1983, and Frank's messages of support, and then sympathy when in 1987 I lost in Dulwich after three recounts, were uplifting; he was the first to back me when the by-election in Vauxhall took place in 1989. I had fought a gruelling campaign with the local party which at that time was in the control of the very hard left. On arriving in the Commons Frank gave me good advice about how to handle the 'wreckers' as he call them: 'Don't give an inch at general committee meetings, no matter what they throw at you.'

He suggested I become a member of the Social Security Committee, which he chaired, and here I was to see his brilliant way of getting the very best from witnesses on so many important matters. He always left the room to bring them in personally rather than waiting for a clerk to do so, and even when he was probing incisively he showed a kindness, understanding that some witnesses were very nervous. I loved his willingness to say publicly and forthrightly what many others wanted to say but wouldn't for fear of upsetting the Labour leadership.

After much persuasion from fellow members he agreed to his select committee's first overseas visit. He wasn't looking forward to the long flight to Australia and New Zealand and was so worried about sleeping that he took a sleeping pill despite me telling him it was much too early on the flight. Unsurprisingly as we all tucked into our lovely dinner on the plane he fell asleep and missed the meal. A few hours later when we all had settled down, he woke up and started talking loudly about being hungry. We were not amused!

When he was appointed minister in 1997 by Tony Blair he asked me to be his Parliamentary Private Secretary (PPS). For some reason the Chief Whip delayed and delayed, and then called me in to say that they would rather I was a PPS to someone else and made suggestions that my future career prospects would be better served elsewhere than with Frank. Needless to say that made both of us quite angry, and so my appointment went ahead.

Most Sunday evenings Frank would come for supper in my flat overlooking Tower Bridge. Usually the same friends were there, and those who used the word 'ascetic' to describe him might have been surprised to see the speed and singlemindedness with which he could devour the better part of the box of Roses chocolates, with which he always arrived over many years.

Relaxing on those occasions, I treasured the way he would express himself with disarming and incisive frankness on political developments of the day as well as on world affairs. Indeed, sometimes he made what would be seen as outrageous remarks. As a voracious reader and a devout Christian he drew on a wide range of knowledge and historical context, and his views were informed by an understanding of the lives of people in the UK, albeit particularly of those in his Birkenhead constituency.

He was bold and original in his thinking, with his fine mind informed by decades of detailed research, most notably on the many ways in which poverty affects lives, and his recognition that the benefit and social welfare system can sometimes be as much a hindrance as a help if, through dependency, it inadvertently leads to poverty of ambition or opportunity. He understood from close engagement how destructive such factors can be to families and to personal development, and frequently used examples of his own constituents. His tussles with Harriet Harman were regular, particularly when he was trying to get the PM to take seriously his radical suggestions on welfare reform. He was always polite and never publicly showed his real anger at being blocked by Gordon Brown. Even in the turbulent hours before he decided to resign, when Blair had wanted to shuffle him, he didn't rage but rather just became more and more determined. When we walked out of the department for the last time, I remember his stoicism. It wasn't the trappings of office he missed – it was the opportunity to change policy and people's lives.

His bravery and courage were physical as well as intellectual, as when he stood up to the infiltration and intimidation from Militant in Birkenhead – and won. Both of us had faced great unpleasantness and opposition from within our local parties, which never reflected the widespread support we received over decades from the local electorate – with increased majorities as evidence.

Frank and I shared positions on so many important political matters. He was ahead of his time in wanting to see controls on immigration and we both opposed the UK allowing new EU members immediate free movement access to the UK. His support for withdrawal from the European Union surprised many, but a few years earlier he had signed up to the Labour campaign calling for a referendum on the issue.

Visiting Northern Ireland with me on a number of occasions he was an advocate of strengthening the Union and never really believed in devolution or indeed local mayors. On my visits during his long illness he always asked me for an update on the campaign against the Protocol.[1] His logical thinking and the clarity with which he expressed himself – whether writing or speaking – made him a formidable opponent for those with whose views or policies he disagreed.

Outwardly dour, Frank had a dry wit and humour and this made it fun to be with him whether on political matters or socially. Indeed he had a very recognisable laugh that echoed round the Chamber on many occasions. He was devoted to his mother, and when she became frail she moved into the Little Sisters of the Poor home in Vauxhall where he visited almost every day walking back from the Commons. Of course the staff all loved him, and he would often come back with a message for me about some problem they were having with Lambeth Council.

Since 2020 we both were independent active peers in the House of Lords but sadly his time there was short. The fulsome tributes that flowed from across the political spectrum speak eloquently to Frank as an upholder of principle and honour, attributes that have sadly become rarer amongst MPs since his first election in 1979. He never changed, and I will always be grateful for his loyal friendship and the happy times we enjoyed. His legacy on welfare will be in the history books, but it was Frank as a kind principled man with no airs and graces who will be remembered most.

---

1. The Protocol on Ireland/Northern Ireland, intended to protect the EU single market, while avoiding post-Brexit imposition of a 'hard border'.

# Charles, Lord Moore
## IMPRESSIONS OF FRANK FIELD

Frank was known and respected as a Christian in public life but was nevertheless quite private about his faith. As in all important matters, he was at once outspoken in his opinions and reticent about his inner being. What was his faith?

My impression was that he had been consistently religious from his boyhood and that his faith had been shaped and fortified by Church itself. Indeed, with his dark hair, slender form, and ascetic expression (when not suddenly transformed by his wicked grin), he physically resembled a devout youth in an Italian renaissance painting. He was not at all one of those people who speak of themselves as 'spiritual but not religious'. Church, first encountered through St Nicholas, an embodiment of the sacramental Anglo-Catholic tradition of the Church of England, in his Chiswick childhood, meant a great deal to him. He loved the beauty of holiness, and found its best verbal expression in the Book of Common Prayer: he and I were both patrons of the Prayer Book Society. I think he believed in T.S. Eliot's formulation, that 'The communication of the dead is tongued with fire beyond the language of the living.'

Brian and Rachel Griffiths, who knew Frank so well and helped him so much in later years, told me of the regular Sunday ritual. Frank would return to London from his Birkenhead constituency in the afternoon and meet them in time for evensong at Holy Trinity, Sloane Street, the handsome and well-ordered Arts and Crafts church that was to be the scene of his funeral. Dinner often followed. The church is sufficiently 'high' to include the Catholic service of Benediction after evensong, and Frank, perhaps not seeing himself as 'Romish', used to leave before it began. Brian and Rachel, however, though definitely low-church themselves, loved the service and eventually persuaded Frank to stay with them for it. He became a devotee; but I do not think he could ever have become a Roman Catholic: he was too thoroughly English to think that way.

Indeed, it was their common Englishness that attracted Frank to Margaret Thatcher in matters of religion. Her Methodist background was unlike his Anglican one, but he loved her memory for good hymns, usually Protestant ones, because, as he told me, 'Hymns kept the faith alive over the centuries when the clergy weren't doing their job.'

I think he also shared with Mrs Thatcher a vision of England as a place – or formerly a place – of good Christian social order, as transmitted to him by his own beloved mother, a pillar of working-class Toryism, to whom he most successfully introduced the first woman prime minister. Mrs Thatcher famously said, 'There is no such thing as a society' and was much criticised for it, but Frank knew the sentences with which she followed up that remark, about how 'individual people and their families', not some abstract political concept, compose society. Far from repudiating the notion of society, she was keen to reassert its foundational principles, and the responsibilities these laid upon everyone. Although Frank came from a left-wing redistributionist approach to wealth, he respected what he saw as Mrs Thatcher's belief in the duty and dignity of labour and her wish to extend the opportunities of ownership to those whose ancestors had never known them. He and she were surprisingly close in their respect for the social contract and contributory principles devised in the middle of the twentieth century by people like Beveridge. They protested not at the idea of state welfare, but at its later corruption.

It was touching that the Labour MP and the arch-Conservative were so close (and how considerate Mrs Thatcher was in trying to hide their friendship from those in his party who might attack him for it). Being much churchier than she, Frank was full of high-quality Church gossip and would privately advise her on whom to favour in Church appointments, advice to which she listened carefully, if cautiously. But I think what each liked about the other was not so much politics, ecclesiastical or secular, as plain sincerity and a sense of mission.

When young, Frank developed his adult ideas about Christianity and society, drawing on the Idealism of T.H. Green, but favouring explicitly Christian beliefs over detached respect for religion. He was an admirer of Charles Gore's once-famous collection of essays by several Anglo-Catholic theologians, *Lux Mundi*, whose title suggests its interest in Jesus as a presence in the life of the modern world. Thought from that Victorian era inspired Frank more than the later teachings of Christian socialism, which he considered naively optimistic about the capacity of the state to guarantee public virtue. Frank believed in the coming of the Kingdom of God and was sceptical about human beings who claimed they could manage this by their own efforts. His views thus combined left-wing social concern and suspicion of laissez-faire with moral conservatism and a tolerant awareness of human failings. His was an incarnational, not an other-worldly religion. It inspired his extraordinary devotion to his constituents over so many years, and his constant projects for charity and social reform.

I am sure Frank would have repudiated the idea that he was a holy man, but he was a man of prayer. If others asked to pray with him, he would always say yes. Some of the clergy, notably Dorrien Davies, now Bishop of St Davids, would assist his prayer life, as would Father Nicholas Spicer. At Eastertide 2024, the word went out that Frank's life was nearing its end. A call reached Brian and Rachel Griffiths en route to their house in Wales. They turned back to London and arranged for a priest, Mike Neville of St Simon Zelotes, Chelsea, to come to Frank's hospital bed, in a busy public ward in St Mary's, Paddington. It seemed fitting that Frank was dying there, interceded for amidst the bustle of the living. In fact, he did not die then, but lived for a month more.

What drove Frank so hard in his religious life and therefore in his worldly one? He confided in friends that though he did not doubt the truth of Christianity, he had always lacked the personal sense of 'assurance', that experience which brings so much comfort and is particularly treasured by Protestants. He knew that Jesus was God and believed in His love, but he did not quite feel, perhaps, that Jesus had made Himself known, personally, to him – almost as if they had been at the same party but had not been introduced. His search for this assurance drove him forward.

For the reception of his body, and for his funeral, Frank chose hymns – 'Hark, the Glad Sound' and 'Lo! He Comes With Clouds Descending' – usually associated with Advent, rather than with death. Perhaps he cherished the idea of Jesus's coming, making Himself known in the ordinary world through which Frank had been a lifelong pilgrim.

# Nicholas, Lord Soames

## IMPRESSIONS OF FRANK FIELD

One of the greatest pleasures in Parliament, if you are lucky enough to have them, are the many cross-party friendships. Quite often they are initiated by working together on a particular issue, or on a select committee, or perhaps being parliamentary neighbours. But the most natural ones are those that are the most unexpected.

I became a Member of Parliament in 1983 and was privileged to join a number of Dining Clubs. It was at the Blue Chip that I had many friends who all appeared to be great friends of Frank Field's. I think we were probably introduced by Robert Salisbury who was a close friend and great admirer of Frank's.

I immediately found him an immensely congenial companion and completely exceptional in his own party, which was at the time fractious and ridden with schism.

In particular, I greatly admired his courage in fighting off the constant intimidation in his Constituency Labour Party from Militant, and his fortitude was already something of a legend among my friends and contemporaries.

It was only really in later Parliaments that we came together to work on a number of issues, in particular on immigration. Frank's views were far-seeing; he saw before many other people the great hazard of uncontrolled immigration, and together with Sir Andrew Green, the former senior British diplomat who became a friend of us both, we established Migration Watch.

I like to believe that Migration Watch was the first serious attempt to get the true facts and figures of the numbers of people coming here, the likely impact that they would have, and the need for a proper and frank discussion about such a grave matter.

He was quite literally without fear. He had endless rows with his own party about which he was nearly always right. He sometimes single-handedly seemed to be championing the fight against poverty.

His views on poverty were informed by his Christianity and by the everyday experiences of his constituents in Birkenhead, a town left in an appalling state after the collapse of its docks and shipyards.

He had a remarkable relationship with Mrs Thatcher when she was Prime Minister, and afterwards too he had access to her not normally granted even to a member of her own party. They both shared a firm conviction that self-reliance and self-improvement were by far the best way ahead. He said of her that she was the first prime minister since Gladstone to address the big moral questions.

He was an exceptional Chairman of the Work and Pensions Select Committee. High-minded, deeply principled and fearless – he was not a man to suffer fools when they appeared in front of him.

Frank loved history, which informed his knowledge and the historical context of his views. He would often drop into my office and sit down just to have a friendly chat. In later days we profoundly disagreed about Brexit without ever having a cross word. My secretary and others were devoted to him. Frank always had remarkably good people working for him and he was always a real pleasure to deal with.

He suffered his long illness with immense gallantry, fortified by his Christian faith. He was a very dear and good man and I am extremely proud to have been his friend.

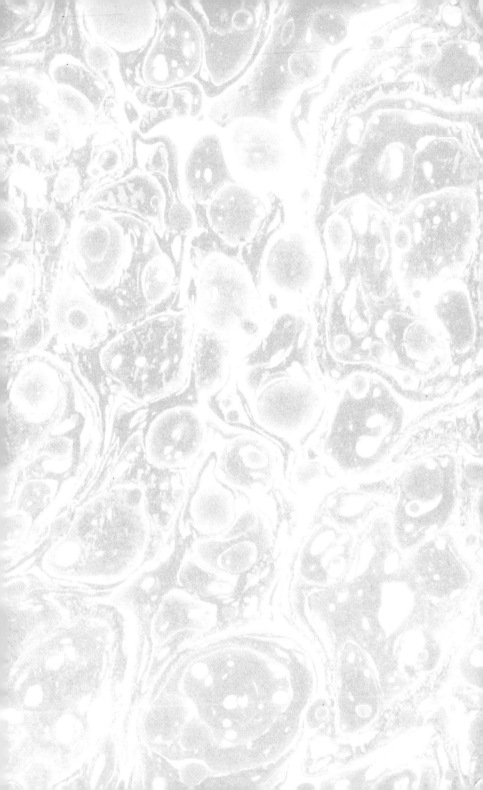